Access to History

General Editor: Keith Rand(

The American Civil War 1861-65

Alan Farmer

Hodder & Stoughton

A MEMBER OF THE HODDER HEADLINE GROUP

The cover illustration shows a portrait of Robert E. Lee (Courtesy of Peter Newark's Pictures)

Some other titles in the series:

The Origins of the American Civil War 1861-65   ISBN 0 340 65869 X
Alan Farmer

The Reconstruction and Effects of the American   ISBN 0 340 67935 2
Civil War 1865-77
Alan Farmer

The USA and the Cold War 1945-63   ISBN 0 340 67963 8
Oliver Edwards

Prosperity, Depression and the New Deal   ISBN 0 340 65871 X
Peter Clements

British Library Cataloguing in Publication Data

A catalogue for this title is available from the British Library

ISBN 0-340-65870-3

First published 1996

Impression number   10   9   8   7   6   5   4   3
Year   2005   2004   2003   2002   2001   2000

Copyright © 1996 Alan Farmer

Typeset by Sempringham publishing services, Bedford
Printed in Great Britain for Hodder & Stoughton Educational,
a division of Hodder Headline Plc, 338 Euston Road, London NW1 3BH
by Redwood Books, Trowbridge, Wiltshire

Contents

Preface

To the general reader

Although the *Access to History* series has been designed with the needs of students studying the subject at higher examination levels very much in mind, it also has a great deal to offer the general reader. The main body of the text (i.e. ignoring the Study Guides at the ends of chapters) forms a readable and yet stimulating survey of a coherent topic as studied by historians. However, each author's aim has not merely been to provide a clear explanation of what happened in the past (to interest and inform): it has also been assumed that most readers wish to be stimulated into thinking further about the topic and to form opinions of their own about the significance of the events that are described and discussed (to be challenged). Thus, although no prior knowledge of the topic is expected on the reader's part, she or he is treated as an intelligent and thinking person throughout. The author tends to share ideas and possibilities with the reader, rather than passing on numbers of so-called 'historical truths'.

To the student reader

There are many ways in which the series can be used by students studying History at a higher level. It will, therefore, be worthwhile thinking about your own study strategy before you start your work on this book. Obviously, your strategy will vary depending on the aim you have in mind, and the time for study that is available to you.

If, for example, you want to acquire a general overview of the topic in the shortest possible time, the following approach will probably be the most effective:

1 Read Chapter 1 and think about its contents.
2 Read the 'Making notes' section at the end of Chapter 2 and decide whether it is necessary for you to read this chapter.
3 If it is, read the chapter, stopping at each heading to note down the main points that have been made.
4 Repeat stage 2 (and stage 3 where appropriate) for all the other chapters.

If, however, your aim is to gain a thorough grasp of the topic, taking however much time is necessary to do so, you may benefit from carrying out the same procedure with each chapter, as follows:

1 Read the chapter as fast as you can, and preferably at one sitting.
2 Study the flow diagram at the end of the chapter, ensuring that you understand the general 'shape' of what you have just read.

3 Read the 'Making notes' section (and the 'Answering essay questions' section, if there is one) and decide what further work you need to do on the chapter. In particularly important sections of the book, this will involve reading the chapter a second time and stopping at each heading to think about (and to write a summary of) what you have just read.

4 Attempt the 'Source-based questions' section. It will sometimes be sufficient to think through your answers, but additional understanding will often be gained by forcing yourself to write them down.

When you have finished the main chapters of the book, study the 'Further Reading' section and decide what additional reading (if any) you will do on the topic.

This book has been designed to help make your studies both enjoyable and successful. If you can think of ways in which this could have been done more effectively, please write to tell me. In the meantime, I hope that you will gain greatly from your study of History.

Keith Randell

Acknowledgements

The Publishers would like to thank the following for permission to reproduce illustrations in this volume:

Cover - Robert E. Lee, courtesy of Peter Newark's Pictures. Corbis (UK) Ltd, p. 21 and p. 36; The Trustees of Cambridge University Library p. 32, p. 86 (top) and p. 136 (bottom); Sempringham publishing services p. 121 and p. 136 (top).

The publishers would like to thank the following for permission to reproduce copyright material:

Simon and Schuster for K.M. Stampp (ed.) *The Causes of the Civil War* and Richard Current (ed.) *The Encyclopaedia of the Confederacy* (vol. 1); Oxford University Press for G.R. Evans and E.H. Simpson (eds.) *Far, Far from Home.*

Every effort has been made to trace and acknowledge ownership of copyright. The Publishers will be glad to make suitable arrangements with any copyright holders whom it has not been possible to contact.

CHAPTER 1

The Start of the War

1 Introduction

The Civil War was, perhaps, the greatest failure in American history. Some 620,000 Americans - 4 per cent of the male population - were to die in the four-year conflict. The blood-letting was similar (proportionally) to Europe's blood-letting in the First World War. Few Europeans regard the First World War as romantic or glorious. Most Americans, however, continue to view their Civil War as something that was noble and heroic. The different way in which the Civil War and the First World War are viewed may have much to do with the issues perceived to rest on their outcome. Few now can see what great issues were at stake in the First World War. But at least two great issues were resolved by the American Civil War: the Union survived; and the slaves were freed.

The Civil War is often seen as the great watershed in American history. The historian/writer Shelby Foote has summarised this quite neatly: before the war the United States were an 'are'; after the war the USA became an 'is'! (Foote might have added that during the war the USA could well have become a 'was'.) Many historians see the war - and its results - as the second American Revolution. (The first was the American War of Independence.) The perceived importance of the war, coupled with the romance that still surrounds it, has led to the publication of a colossal number of scholarly books and articles. No topic in American history has had so much written about it.

Historians have a massive amount of raw material to interpret. Mid-nineteenth-century America was a literate society and an abundance of written sources survive - letters, diaries, journals, newspapers, autobiographies and official documents. There are also hundreds of thousands of photographs, as many sketches and paintings by contemporary artists, hundreds of songs, and tons of artefacts of every description. But the wealth of material does not mean that the Civil War is easy to understand. The poet Walt Whitman, who served as a nurse during the war, thought: 'Future years will never know the seething hell, the black infernal background, the countless minor scenes and interiors of the secession war, and it is best they should not'. The real war, he thought, would never get in books. Historians, it must be said, have done their best to ensure that the 'real' war has got into books. But historians, being historians, have fiercely debated virtually every aspect of the war. This book can only scratch the surface of some of the (many) controversies.

2 The Causes of the War

The causes of the war have been - and continue to be - keenly debated. (For more detail on the causes, you should read the companion volume to this book, *The Origins of the American Civil War*.) During the war few people on either side would have dissented from Abraham Lincoln's statement in 1865 that slavery 'was somehow, the cause of the war'. In March 1861 Alexander Stephens, the Confederate Vice President, also emphasised the importance of slavery, declaring:

> 1 The new Constitution has put at rest forever all the agitating
>   questions relating to our peculiar institution - African slavery as it
>   exists among us - the proper status of the negro in our form of
>   civilisation. This was the immediate cause of the late rupture and
> 5 the present revolution ... The prevailing ideas entertained by ...
>   most of the leading statesmen at the time of the formation of the
>   old Constitution were that the enslavement of the African was in
>   violation of the laws of nature and that it was wrong in principle,
>   socially, morally and politically ... Those ideas, however, were
> 10 fundamentally wrong. They rested upon the assumption of the
>   equality of races. This was an error ... Our new Government is
>   founded upon exactly the opposite ideas; its foundations are laid,
>   its cornerstone rests, upon the great truth that the negro is not
>   equal to the white man; that slavery, subordination to the superior
> 15 race, is his natural and moral condition.

For half a century or so after 1865, most historians regarded slavery as the main cause of the war. In 1913 James Ford Rhodes, the foremost Civil War historian of his day, declared that 'of the American Civil War it may safely be asserted that there was a single cause, slavery'. But many historians then - and since - disagreed strongly with this view. The Confederate President Jefferson Davis insisted in his memoirs that the Southern states had seceded and gone to war not to protect slavery but to vindicate state sovereignty. Southerners, Davis claimed, had fought solely 'for the defence of an inherent, unalienable right ... to withdraw from a Union which they had, as sovereign communities, voluntarily entered ... The existence of African servitude was in no wise the cause of the conflict, but only an incident'. Many Southerners accepted this explanation and viewed the conflict as a war of Northern aggression against Southern rights.

In the 1920s many historians saw clashes between economic interest groups and classes as the central theme of history. The war, in the eyes of some 'progressive' historians was a contest between plantation agriculture, on the one hand, and industrialising capitalism on the other. It was not primarily a conflict between North and South: 'Merely by the accidents of climate, soil and geography was it a sectional struggle', wrote Charles Beard, a leading progressive historian. In Beard's view, the war was not a contest between slavery and freedom. Slavery just happened to be the labour system of plantation agriculture, just as wage labour happened to be the system of Northern industry. According to Beard the real issues dividing Northern manufacturers from Southern planters were the tariff, government subsidies to transportation and manufacturing, and public land sales. Many Southerners were delighted with this progressive interpretation. The Confederacy, it seemed, fought not only for the principle of state rights and self-government but also for the preservation of a stable, agrarian civilisation in the face of the grasping ambitions of Northern businessmen. Perhaps it was no coincidence that this interpretation emerged at much the same time as *Gone With the Wind* was one of the most popular literary and cinematic successes of all time.

During the 1940s another interpretation, usually called 'revisionism', dominated the work of academic historians. The revisionists denied that sectional conflicts between North and South - whether over slavery, state rights, or industry versus agriculture - were genuinely divisive. In the view of Avery Craven and James Randell (the two giants of revisionism), far more united than divided the two sections. The free and slave states had coexisted peacefully under the same Constitution since 1787. White Americans shared the same language, legal system, political culture, religious values and history. Most also had similar racist views, accepting without question that African Americans were inferior to whites. Most white Northerners were as committed to white supremacy as (virtually all) white Southerners. In the eyes of the revisionists, the differences that separated North and South could and should have been accommodated peacefully. The Civil War, therefore, was not an irrepressible conflict, as earlier generations had called it, but 'The Repressible Conflict' as Craven titled one of his books. The war was brought on not by genuine issues but by extremists on both sides - rabble-rousing abolitionists and Southern 'fire-eaters' - who whipped up emotions and hatreds for their own partisan purposes. The passions they aroused got out of hand because politicians of the time lacked the skill of previous generations and failed to reach a compromise. The result, according to the revisionists, was a tragic, unnecessary war that accomplished nothing that could not have been achieved by negotiation. Of course, any compromise in 1861 would have left slavery in place. But revisionists argued that slavery would have soon died peacefully of natural causes.

Historiography, however, has now come full circle. Most historians today agree with Lincoln's assertion that slavery was, 'somehow', the cause of the war. The state rights, progressive, and revisionist schools are presently dormant if not actually dead. While the agricultural South and the industrialising North did have different economic interests, the Civil War was not fought over issues of the tariff or banks or agrarianism versus industrialism. Such issues had existed throughout American history, often generating a great deal more friction than they did in the 1850s. Moreover, the image of an agrarian South facing an urban North must always be qualified. In 1860, fewer than 25 per cent of Northerners actually lived in 'towns' with more than 2,500 people. Nor was the war the result of false issues trumped up by fanatics. It was fought over profound, intractable problems that Americans, both North and South, believed went to the heart of their society. Slavery lay at the root of the antagonism. To say that 'only' slavery divided the North from the South is akin to saying that 'only' religion divides people in Northern Ireland. Slavery was the sole institution not shared by North and South. The so-called 'peculiar institution' defined the South, permeating almost every aspect of its life. In 1858 a prominent - and relatively moderate - Northern politician, Senator William Seward of New York, declared that the social systems of slave labour and free labour 'are more than incongruous - they are incompatible'. The friction between them is 'an irreconcilable conflict between opposing and enduring forces, and it means that the United States must and will, sooner or later, become either entirely a slaveholding nation, or entirely a free-labour nation'. By 1860 most Southerners agreed with Seward that an irreconcilable conflict had split the country into two hostile cultures.

Slaves were the principal form of wealth in the South. The market value of its 4,000,000 slaves in 1860 was $3 billion - more than the value of land and cotton. Slave labour made it possible for the South to grow 75 per cent of the world's cotton, which in turn constituted half of all the USA's exports. But slavery was much more than an economic system. It was a means of maintaining racial control and white supremacy. Only 25 per cent of Southern whites actually owned slaves in 1860. But the vast majority of non-slaveholding whites supported the peculiar institution. Many white farmers aspired to become slaveholders themselves They also feared what would happen if the slaves were freed. By the mid-nineteenth century most white Southerners saw slavery as a positive good for black and white alike - essential to the peace, safety and prosperity of their section.

Southerners were spurred into defending slavery by the rise of militant abolitionism in the North after 1830. William Lloyd Garrison, Frederick Douglass and a host of other eloquent crusaders branded slavery as both a sin and a violation of the principles of liberty on which the USA had been founded. Although few Northerners supported racial equality, the belief that slavery was unjust, obsolete and unrepublican entered mainstream Northern politics. Most Northerners extolled the virtues of a free-labour ideology. Slavery, it seemed, prevented poor and middling whites from competing equally with slave planters, degraded the concept of labour, and helped block social mobility.

It was the issue of slavery expansion, rather than its mere existence, that polarised the nation. In the mid-1850s a new Northern political party, the Republican party, emerged, pledged to stop the further spread of slavery. The containment of slavery should ensure that ultimately it withered and died. That was just what Southerners feared. The Northern population, helped by immigration, was already growing at a much faster rate than the South. The North, therefore, had a majority in the House of Representatives. New Western free states would also give the free states a greater majority in the Senate. Ultimately, this could threaten the peculiar institution. Worried by the population imbalance, Southerners increasingly accepted the view that sovereignty lay in the individual states and that in certain circumstances secession might well be a justified process.

For most of the 1850s the South managed to retain control of the presidency, Congress and the Supreme Court. This was because Southerners dominated the Democrat party. This party continued to win considerable support in the North, largely from Irish and German Catholics and from farmers (often of Southern stock) in Midwestern states like Illinois. Although the Democrat Presidents Franklin Pierce (1853-7) and James Buchanan (1857-61) were Northerners, they held pro-Southern views. This - somewhat unnatural - Southern political dominance convinced many Northerners that there was a 'Slave Power' conspiracy at work, subverting the country's values and institutions. By 1856 the Republican party, committed to opposing the 'Slave Power' and slave expansion, had become the strongest party in the North and carried most Northern states in the 1856 presidential election. Nevertheless, James Buchanan won the election. His presidency was dogged by the situation in the territory of Kansas. Open warfare between pro and anti-slavery settlers in Kansas spilled over into Congress. Events in Kansas divided Northerners from Southerners, so much so that in 1858 many Northern Democrats followed the lead of Senator Stephen Douglas and broke with Buchanan.

In 1859 the abolitionist John Brown, viewed by some at the time and since as a hero and by others (more accurately) as a murderer and a lunatic, led an extraordinary raid to seize the Federal armoury at Harper's Ferry in Virginia. Once in possession of the arms, he hoped to spark off a chain reaction of slave uprisings throughout the South. His wild dreams came to nothing. The raid was a failure. Most of Brown's followers were killed. Brown, himself, was captured, and hung. But the Harper's Ferry raid did succeed in sending shock waves through the South. A slave revolt was white Southerners' greatest fear. Southerners equated Brown with all abolitionists and abolitionists with the 'Black Republicans'.

In 1860 the Democrat Party, like almost every other institution in America, split North and South. Northern Democrats nominated Stephen Douglas for President. Southern Democrats nominated John Breckinridge. This helped ensure the election of the Republican candidate Abraham Lincoln who carried every Northern state. Only a handful of Southerners voted for Lincoln. For many Southerners, Lincoln's election was the writing on the wall. It seemed they had lost control of the government. The fact that the North had elected a President who believed slavery a 'monstrous injustice' that should be 'placed in the course of ultimate extinction' seemed both a threat and an affront to Southern honour. So, over the winter of 1860-1 seven lower South states voted to secede from the Union. South Carolina was the first to go in December 1860. Mississippi, Florida, Alabama, Georgia, Louisiana and Texas soon followed. Delegates from these states met at Montgomery, Alabama in February 1861 and formed the Confederate States of America. The Montgomery convention also elected Jefferson Davis, Mississippi Senator, as Confederate President.

However, eight upper South slave states did not immediately secede. They hoped for a compromise that would preserve the Union. But no room for compromise could be found. Lincoln and the Republicans were committed to preventing slavery expansion: the Confederate states were committed to secession.

Secession did not necessarily mean war. Lincoln's government could have allowed the 'erring sisters' to 'depart in peace'. But most Northerners were not willing to accept the dismemberment of the Union. They believed that toleration of disunion would end the great experiment in republican self-government and create a precedent to be invoked by disaffected minorities in the future. 'If the minority have the right to break up the Government at pleasure, because they have not had their way, there is an end of all government', wrote a Cincinnati editor, a view echoed by many Northern newspapers. Even President Buchanan regarded secession as illegal. But, as a 'lame duck' president after November 1860, he was not prepared to do anything about it. Lincoln, however, made it clear in his inaugural address in March 1861, that he was determined to maintain the Union. By adopting a policy of 'masterly inactivity' Lincoln hoped to allow passions to cool, enabling Unionists to regain influence in the lower South.

But this hope was doomed from the start. Genuine Unionists had all but disappeared in the Confederate states. Moreover, the new President found himself facing an immediate crisis which meant that time was not on his side. The seceded states had taken over most Federal property within their borders. But a few forts still remained under Federal control, most conspicuously Fort Sumter, on an island in Charleston harbour. Lincoln had pledged himself to maintain it. Action was necessary in the spring of 1861 because the garrison (of some 80 men) was short of supplies. Lincoln determined to resupply the fort and told the Confederate government of his intentions.

President Jefferson Davis considered it dishonourable that the Union flag was still flying in Charleston harbour. Spurred on by Confederate public opinion, Davis determined to assert Confederate sovereignty, confident that the outbreak of war would force the upper South states to join the Confederacy. As a Federal relief expedition approached Charleston, Davis ordered General Beauregard, commander of the Confederate troops at Charleston, to open fire on Fort Sumter. Artillery fire commenced at 4.30 am on 12 April. It ended 33 hours later. During the bombardment Confederate artillery fired 4,000 rounds and the Union guns in Sumter replied with a 1,000. Amazingly, there were no fatalities. With the fort on fire and no hope of relief, the Union garrison surrendered. The crucial fact was that the Confederacy had fired the first shots. The reaction in the North was similar to that in the USA after the Japanese attack on Pearl Harbor in 1941. Northerners were now united in opposition to the Confederacy and set on war.

Lincoln immediately called upon those states remaining in the Union for troops. The upper South states now had to commit themselves. Virginia, Tennessee, Arkansas and North Carolina, deciding that slavery was their cornerstone, voted to join the Confederacy. Virginia's decision was crucial. It was the largest-populated slave state and the most industrial. The moving of the Confederate capital from Montgomery to Richmond (state capital of Virginia) in May 1861 was an acknowledgement of Virginia's importance.

In 1861 Lincoln was not pledged to end slavery: he was simply pledged to preserve the Union. The Confederate states were fighting for

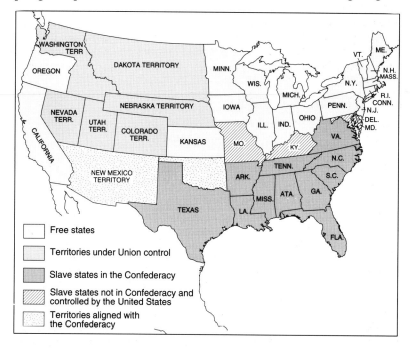

The Divided Nation: Confederacy versus Union 1861

the right to self-determination. Nationalism was thus the immediate cause of the Civil War. Relatively few Northerners in 1861 were fighting to end slavery. However, it was slavery which had led to the sectional impasse between North and South. Differences arising from the slavery issue led to the secession of the Southern states. While the Confederacy claimed its justification to be the protection of state rights, in truth, it was primarily one state right - the right to preserve slavery - that impelled the Confederate states' separation. For this right many Southerners were prepared to fight to the death. While few Northerners were willing to fight to emancipate the slave, most were prepared to fight to save the Union. The slave issue meant they had to fight to save the Union.

Abraham Lincoln in March 1865 gave a succinct account of what he saw as the main causes of the war.

1 One eighth of the whole population was coloured slaves, not distributed generally over the Union, but localised in the southern part of it. These slaves constituted a peculiar and powerful interest. All knew that this interest was somehow the cause of the war. To
5 strengthen, perpetuate, and extend this interest was the object for which the insurgents would rend the Union even by war, while the government claimed no right to do more than to restrict the territorial enlargement of it. Neither party expected for the war the magnitude or the duration which it has already attained. Neither
10 anticipated that the cause of the conflict might cease with or even before the conflict itself should cease. Each looked for an easier triumph and a result less fundamental and astounding.

3 What to Call the Conflict?

Since 1861 Americans have argued over a name for the conflict. By far the most popular name today is 'The Civil War'. Both sides used the term throughout the four-year struggle. The conflict was indeed a civil war in states like Missouri and Kentucky where brother sometimes did fight brother. However, this was not the norm. The reality was that the war was waged by two separate geographical regions: most Northerners were on the Union side and most Southerners were on the Confederate side. Civil War, therefore, is not a totally satisfactory title. Moreover, the term implies that two different sections of the nation were fighting for control of a single government when in actual fact the Confederacy was seeking to exist independently.

After 1865 Southerners frequently called the conflict, 'The War between the States'. However, this title was rather cumbersome and not quite correct: the contest was waged not by states but by two organised governments - the Union and the Confederacy. Northerners sometimes referred to the conflict as 'The War of the Rebellion'. This term is also cumbersome. Moreover, the conflict was more than a rebellion: it lasted four years and was fought by two governments respecting the rules of war. Other terms which have occasionally been used to describe the conflict (each of which has a connotation that offers a different explanation or account of what the struggle was about) include 'The War for Southern Independence', 'The War for Secession', 'The War against Slavery', 'War of the Sections' and 'The War for Nationality'. It should be said that virtually everyone now calls the war the Civil War. This book will be no exception.

4 Why Did the War Last so Long?

Tens of thousands of Northerners and Southerners flocked to the colours in the spring of 1861. Most anticipated one glorious battle and a triumphant return home. But instead of a summer frolic, the war turned into a four-year bloodbath. This was partly the result of the changed nature of warfare (see Chapter 2). But it was also to do with the fact that both North and South had strengths and weaknesses which tended to offset those of the other side. This is not to say that both sides were equally balanced. On paper - and in reality - the North was far stronger than the South. However, the Confederacy did have certain advantages which its leaders hoped - and expected - to be able to exploit.

a) Northern Advantages

From the start the North had a considerable manpower advantage. There were 22,000,000 people in the North compared with only 9,000,000 in the South (of whom only 5,500,000 were whites). The Confederacy could probably draw on around 2,000,000 men of military age. In contrast, the Union could call on nearly 7,000,000 white males and, although at first reluctant to use them, could also rely on hundreds of thousands of black Americans.

Although still overwhelmingly rural in 1861, the North had a much greater industrial capacity (see Table 1). In 1860 Northern states produced 97 per cent of the United States' firearms, 94 per cent of its pig iron, and 90 per cent of its boots and shoes. The North had six times as many factories as the South and ten times its productive capacity. The South had only one city - New Orleans - with a population greater than 50,000 people. The North had twice as many miles of railway track as the South and plenty of skilled workers and engineers to maintain its railway network. (Those who predicted in 1861 that it was beyond the power of the North to conquer the South, overlooked what the railway might do.) Even in agriculture the North enjoyed an edge. It had more horses, cows and sheep and produced over 80 per cent of the country's wheat and oats. The North would have no difficulty feeding, clothing and arming its troops - unlike the Confederacy.

The Confederacy hoped to make good its lack of basic materials by trading with Europe, especially Britain. But from the start of the war the North ruled the waves and was able to impose an increasingly tight blockade. As well as blockading the South, the North could use its naval strength to attack the Confederate coast and threaten its main ports. This meant that the Confederacy had to disperse its already inadequate resources. Moreover, the Union also enjoyed naval supremacy on the 'inland sea' - the Mississippi and its tributaries.

It has sometimes been claimed that, compared with the South, the North lacked military experience. This was not true. The majority of men in the US regular army remained loyal to the Union. So did two-thirds of the officers. This was not surprising. Between 1820 and 1860 nearly two-thirds of all the graduates at West Point, the United States' major military academy, had been Northerners. The Union, therefore, had a stronger pool of military experience to call on than the Confederacy.

The North was further aided by the fact that four slave states, containing some 2,000,000 people, remained loyal to the Union. There was never any likelihood that Delaware would secede. Less than 2 per cent of its population were slaves and its economic ties were with the North. Maryland was another matter. Important geographically (because of its proximity to Washington), many Marylanders were

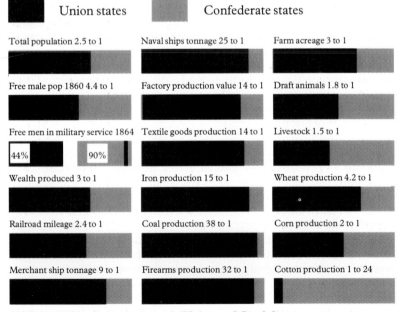

Table 1: Comparative resources in Union and Confederate states

pro-Confederate. In April 1861 there was a serious riot in Baltimore. Union soldiers passing through the town on their way to defend Washington were attacked by pro-Confederate townspeople. Four soldiers and twelve civilians were killed - the first fatalities of the war. There seemed a real possibility that Maryland would secede. But Lincoln, helped by the pro-Union Maryland governor, took strong action. Stretching the constitution to its limits (and probably beyond), he sent in Union troops, temporarily suspended the writ of habeas corpus, and allowed the arrest of suspected trouble-makers. Lincoln's tough measures helped save Maryland for the Union. In June 1861 elections in Maryland were won by Unionist candidates and the state legislature voted against secession. During the war some 30,000 white and (eventually) 9,000 black Marylanders fought for the North. Some 20,000 Marylanders fought for the Confederacy.

Kentucky, the birthplace of both Lincoln and Davis, was even more important than Maryland. 'I think to lose Kentucky is nearly the same as to lose the whole game', thought Lincoln. The state was deeply divided. Governor Beriah Magoffin leaned to the South but most of Kentucky's legislators were opposed to secession. At first the state attempted to remain neutral. Governor Magoffin rejected calls for recruits from both sides and warned both governments to keep out of Kentucky. Lincoln, aware that a false move on his part could easily drive the state into the opposing camp, took no direct action. Instead he relied on patience, tact and backstage manoeuvring. While paying (apparent) respect for the integrity of Kentucky, his government supplied arms to Unionists within the state. Kentucky's precarious neutrality was short-lived. In September 1861 Confederate forces (ill-advisedly) occupied Columbus. The Kentucky legislature, angered by this overt action, determined to adhere to the Union. Union forces were quickly ordered into Kentucky and soon controlled most of the state. During the war some 50,000 Kentucky whites and 24,000 Kentucky blacks fought for the Union; 35,000 Kentucky whites fought for the South.

In the spring of 1861 it seemed likely that Missouri, the most heavily populated state west of the Mississippi, would join the Confederacy. A large part of Missouri's population were of Southern origin and the state governor, was pro-Confederate. In June 1861 he called for 50,000 volunteers to defend the state against Federal invasion. But there was also considerable Unionist support, especially from Missouri's large German population, and despite initial military setbacks, Unionists kept control of most of the state. During the war some 80,000 whites and 8,000 blacks from Missouri fought for the Union. Thirty thousand Missourians joined the Confederate army and thousands more became 'irregulars', fighting a bloody guerilla war against the Unionists.

The fact that Maryland, Kentucky and Missouri did not declare wholeheartedly for the Confederacy was crucial. The three states would have added 45 per cent to the Confederacy's white population and 80 per cent to its manufacturing capacity. The Confederacy would also have gained important strategic advantages, including the highly defensible Ohio river.

Nor were all the people within the eleven Confederate states committed to the Confederate cause. Pockets of Unionism existed, especially in the Appalachian Mountains. The Confederacy suffered a major set back when West Virginia (which had voted overwhelmingly against secession) seceded from Virginia. West Virginia was soon under Unionist control and allowed to become a separate state. (It was admitted to the Union in 1863). Tennessee was also divided. Senator Andrew Johnson remained loyal to the Union and the eastern part of the state was essentially Unionist. During the war over 30,000 white Tennesseans fought for the North.

To offset its shortfall in numbers, the Confederate economic war effort was heavily dependent on slave labour. But slaves were always a potential fifth column within the Confederacy. (Many white Southerners feared a mass slave revolt.) Throughout the war, there was a steady flow of blacks fleeing to the Northern armies and offering their services to the Union.

b) Confederate Advantages

Given the North's advantage in numbers and industrial capacity, the odds were stacked heavily against the South. But war is not just about numbers or productive capacity. Geographical factors are important. So too are courage, organisational skill and leadership. In 1861 most Southerners, and most European observers, were confident that the Confederacy would triumph. Even after the war, many prominent Southerners were convinced that the Confederacy should have won. 'No people ever warred for independence,' said General Beauregard, 'with more relative advantages than the Confederacy'.

The sheer size of the Confederacy - 750,000 square miles - was perhaps its greatest asset. Twice the size of the original 13 colonies, it would obviously be difficult to blockade and conquer. Even if Northern armies succeeded in occupying Confederate territory, they would have difficulty holding down a resentful population and maintaining their supply lines. Nor, Richmond apart, was there any obvious centre of gravity. It was unlikely in 1861 that even the capture of Richmond would have forced the Confederacy to surrender. The Confederacy could afford to yield ground and still win the war, simply by wearing down the Northern will to fight.

The Confederacy did not have to invade the North, hold down occupied territory or capture Washington, New York and Boston to win. All it needed to do was defend. Defence, in both strategic and tactical terms, is usually an easier option in war than attack. The fire-power of the rifle-musket (see Chapter 2) certainly meant that battlefield tactics now favoured the defender. The Union had little option but to attack. There was no other way it could reunite the Union. Southerners hoped that Northern public opinion might come to question high losses. If Northern will collapsed, the Confederacy would win by default.

Geography gave the Confederacy an important strategic advantage. The crucial theatre of the war was the land between Washington and Richmond in North Virginia. Here a series of west to east running rivers - the Rappahannock, Rapidan, York, Chickahominy and James - were to provide an effective barrier to Union armies intent on capturing Richmond. The important and fertile Shenandoah Valley ran from the north-east (near Washington) to the south-west - the wrong direction from the North's point of view. Federal forces who marched down the Valley were heading away from Richmond. The Confederates, on the other hand, could use the Valley for striking into the heart of the North, even threatening to capture the capital itself.

The South also had interior lines of communication. In theory this meant that Confederate commanders were in a position to concentrate their dispersed forces against invading Northern armies, using their manpower to maximum effect. President Davis counted on using the Confederacy's railway system to make maximum use of the South's interior lines, concentrating first against one enemy army and then against another before they were able to concentrate in response.

Slavery proved itself a real benefit to the Confederacy in the first year of the war. The fact that slaves could be left to fill production needs on the home front enabled the South to raise more of its white manpower than the Union. Although the Confederacy did not allow slaves to enlist (until 1865), they nevertheless performed many invaluable military tasks - such as transporting goods to the front and building fortifications.

The Confederacy also appeared to have important psychological advantages. Given that most of the war was fought within the Confederacy, Southerners were obviously defending their own land and homes - a fact that perhaps encouraged them to fight that much harder than Northerners who were fighting for the more abstract pursuit of reunion. In 1861 relatively few Southerners questioned the rightness of the Confederate cause. Southern Churches were 100 per cent behind the war, assuring Southerners that they had God on their side. Morale, commitment and enthusiasm were high in the South in 1861.

Most Southerners were confident that man for man they were far better soldiers than Northerners. In the opinion of most contemporary observers, the ante-bellum South seemed to place more emphasis on martial virtues than the North. 'We are a military people,' declared Jefferson Davis in 1861. In 1860 seven of the eight military colleges in the United States (not including West Point and Annapolis) were in slave states. Southerners had fought superbly well in Mexico and before that in the war for Texan independence. It was Southerners who had usually dominated the senior posts in the American army. The elite of the nation's generals had all been Southerners. Most military experts on both sides of the Atlantic assumed that farmers, who knew how to ride and shoot, were naturally better soldiers than industrial workers. Southerners' image of themselves as better soldiers did not necessarily match up to reality. But there is no doubt that the image was good for morale. The fact that many Northerners feared that Southerners were better soldiers helped ensure that the Confederacy began the war with a psychological advantage.

'King Cotton' was assumed to be the Confederacy's great economic weapon. At the very least cotton sales should enable the Confederacy to purchase weapons and supplies from Europe. There was also the strong possibility that Britain might break the Union naval blockade to ensure that cotton supplies got through to its textile mills. This might well lead to war between Britain and the Union.

Although the Confederacy was likely to be outnumbered and outgunned, there were a number of precedents which suggested that a determined 'David' could defeat a seemingly invincible 'Goliath'. Southerners could point to the American War of Independence and the defeat of Britain. They could point to the way that a few valiant Texans had won independence from Mexico in 1836. They could also point to European examples. In the late sixteenth century, for example, the Dutch had successfully broken away from Spain.

Working on '*Introduction: The Start of the War*'

This chapter has two main objectives: to give you some notion of how and why the American Civil War came about; and to give you an understanding of the strengths and weaknesses of both sides, as they appeared in 1861. You do not need to make very detailed notes on how the war came about. However, you do need to have a good grasp of the strengths and weaknesses of the Union and the Confederacy. This will help you understand how the war developed. You should also have a view about which side had the greatest advantage(s) in 1861.

Source-based questions on '*Introduction: The Start of the War*'

1 The Views of Alexander Stephens and Abraham Lincoln
Read the extracts from Stephens' and Lincoln's speeches on page 2 and page 8. Answer the following questions:
a) According to Stephens, what was the main difference between the men who drew up the old Constitution and the men who set up the Confederacy? (3 marks)
b) To what extent - if at all - does Lincoln slant his speech in favour of the Union? (4 marks)
c) On what might Lincoln and Stephens have agreed? (4 marks)

d) On what might they have disagreed? (4 marks)

2 Population and Economic Resources
Examine the statistics on page 10. Answer the following questions:
a) Why might its greater railway mileage be an important advantage for the North? (4 marks)
b) Confederate leaders were aware of these statistics. Does this mean that they were foolish to secede in 1861? (6 marks)

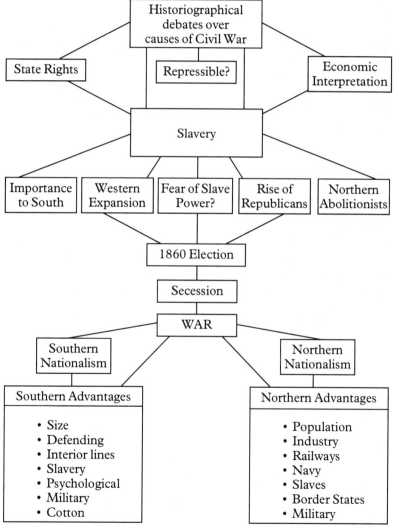

Summary - The Start of the War

CHAPTER 2

The Nature of the War

1 The Situation in 1861

The situation in America in the spring of 1861 was similar to that in Europe in August 1914. Everywhere men, egged on by family, friends and neighbours, rushed to volunteer, their main fear being that the war would be over before they could get a shot at the enemy. Men joined up in such numbers that they could not all be accommodated in the armies and many had to be sent home. Patriotic women, North and South, played a vital role in encouraging men to enlist. Some broke engagements because their fiances did not join up: others sent skirts and female undergarments to shirkers.

Most Americans, forgetting the horrors of Waterloo and the Crimean War, had a romantic image of war - an image that may have come from their perception of the American War of Independence, the newspaper reporting of the Mexican War and/or the fiction of Sir Walter Scott. Few expected a long war. Most Southerners, convinced that one Southerner was better than ten Yankees, were confident that the Confederacy would quickly see off the Union. Northern optimism - given its greater industrial and manpower resources - seemed more soundly based. Most Northerners thought one short campaign and one climactic battle should be enough to suppress the insurrection.

Neither side was prepared for war in 1861. The Union had only a 16,000-strong regular army, most of which was scattered in frontier posts out West. The War Department in Washington totalled only 90 men. President Lincoln had no military (and little administrative) experience. General Winfield Scott, a Virginian who remained loyal to the Union, was the leading 'Northern' general. Although he had once been an excellent soldier, he was 74 years old in 1861 and suffered from dropsy and vertigo. He had no general staff, no carefully prepared strategic plans, no programme for mobilisation and few accurate maps.

In April 1861 Lincoln appealed for 75,000 volunteers to serve for three months. It was soon obvious that this would not be sufficient. In July he asked Congress for 400,000 volunteers to fight for three years: Congress raised the number to 500,000 - far more than could be organised, trained and equipped. Traditionally every able-bodied male, aged 18 to 45, had been required to muster for drill in state militia units once or twice a year. But by the mid-nineteenth century many men had simply stayed away. Several states had abolished militia service altogether: some Western states had never developed a militia system. Most of the Northern state militias that did exist were shambolic.

The Confederacy had to start its military organisation from scratch. President Davis at least had some military experience. Trained at West Point, he had fought in the Mexican War and had been an able Secretary of War in the mid-1850s. The 300 or so Southern army officers who resigned from the regular army to fight for the Confederacy provided a useful pool of talent. Southern state militias, partly as a result of John Brown's raid, were - on balance - better prepared for war than those in the North. The hundreds of volunteer companies which flocked first to Montgomery and then to Richmond, arrived often already uniformed and armed and sometimes even trained, especially those companies that had existed as privately maintained drill units before the war. The Confederate Congress authorised Davis to raise up to 100,000 volunteers in February 1861 for periods of no more than 12-months' service. In May 1861 Congress authorised an additional 400,000 troops, this time for three years' service. Given its limited manufacturing capacity, the South's main problem was equipping the volunteers. In April 1861 it was estimated that there were only about 160,000 muskets in the whole of the South.

Both sides were similarly unprepared at sea. The Union, on paper, had a fleet of some 90 ships in 1861. However, only half of these were in commission and only a handful were immediately ready for blockade duty. Most of the ships were obsolete sailing vessels, designed for deepwater activities rather than service on rivers or inshore. There were only 8,800 men in the Union navy. However, the United States did have

The Naval War 1861-5

a large merchant marine, from which an expanding navy could draw vessels, officers and men. The Confederacy had no navy at all in 1861 and little naval tradition. Although some 300 Southern naval officers resigned their commissions and joined the Confederacy, the likelihood of them finding ships to command seemed minimal. Nearly all the American shipbuilding capacity was in the North.

It is a tribute to the dynamics of mid-nineteenth-century American society that both the Union and the Confederacy could create in months, largely by grass-roots enterprise and vigour, citizen armies of hundreds of thousands of men. But European observers were not particularly impressed: many regarded the American armies with contempt. Moltke, the Prussian Chief of Staff, characterised the military operations of the Civil War as merely, 'Two armed mobs chasing each other around the country, from which nothing could be learned'. There was some justification for this view in 1861. Compared with European professional armies, both the Union and Confederate armies were amateurish - from the top down. Neither Lincoln nor Davis had a recognisable high command structure. Taking whatever advice seemed appropriate, both men had the job of appointing the commanding officers. Political criteria - rather than just military concerns - played an important role in these appointments. A few 'political' generals became first-rate soldiers: but many were totally incompetent.

In 1861 only a minority of 'junior' officers on either side had any military qualifications. Most were appointed by state governors, usually because of their social standing, political influence or personal popularity than for any military experience or skill they might have. Captains and lieutenants were often elected by the men themselves. Few had much idea about military tactics or discipline. The North soon set up military boards to examine officers and to remove those who were found to be incompetent: hundreds were discharged or resigned voluntarily. By 1863 the Union had also ended the practice of electing offices, although this continued in the Confederate army. As the war lengthened, promotion to officer rank on the basis of merit was the norm. Unfortunately this was not always apparent in the camp or on the battlefield. Finding competent non-commissioned officers was also a vexing problem. The result was that inexperienced officers and sergeants ended up training inexperienced troops in outmoded tactics. Men frequently went into battle without even basic training.

Another factor which led to European disdain was the fact that both armies were extremely democratic. The men, unused to military discipline, often questioned orders. Many had little time for army spit and polish. From the start there was widespread insubordination and staggeringly high rates of desertion. The wide variety of uniforms, sported by both sides in 1861, also failed to impress European observers. The most garish were the Zouave regiments whose members wore uniforms similar to those worn by French troops in North Africa -

baggy red pantaloons, white gaiters and fezzes. Not until the second year of the war did Union soldiers virtually all wear blue: in 1861 some wore grey, with unfortunate results at the first battle of Bull Run when Union regiments fired at each other. Throughout the war Southerners wore a wide mixture of assorted clothing: in a sense there was no such thing as a Confederate 'uniform'.

In 1861 most Americans expected the war would be similar to the Mexican War of 1846-8. This had been a war where dash and elan had won the day. Finally 11,000 Americans had marched some 200 miles through Mexico, defeated far larger armies en route and captured Mexico City. Most of the leading commanders on both sides - Lee, 'Stonewall' Jackson, Grant, McClellan - had served in the Mexican War. Most had also been trained at West Point, the United States' main military college. (Of the 60 biggest battles in the Civil War, West Point graduates commanded both armies in 55. In the remaining five a West Pointer commanded one of the opposing armies.) The top officers on both sides, therefore, came from similar backgrounds; most knew each other; they had also learned about war in the same army.

West Point was concerned more with engineering than with grand strategy. What little strategic theory most officers learned tended to be influenced by European ideas, particularly arising from the Napoleonic War. Antoine Henri de Jomini, the principal interpreter of Napoleonic warfare, preached the advantage of movement and manoeuvre and belittled the importance of entrenchments. But Jomini's theories seem to have had limited influence. Some of the best generals (like Grant) admitted to not bothering to read Jomini's work. Interestingly, the West Point - strategic - instructor, Dennis Hart Mahan, emphasised the value of field fortifications and entrenchments more than frontal assaults.

Few officers in 1861 foresaw the scale of the war, the importance of mass citizen armies, the change of tactics that would come about as a result of new weapons, and the dramatic effect that the steam engine would have on movement and supply.

2 Mass Armies

It was obvious from the start that the war would be fought by mass, citizen armies, not by a few, professional troops. Most of the volunteers in 1861 were not attracted by enlistment in the regular army. At no time in the war did the Union regular army reach its modest goal of 42,000 troops and the Confederacy quickly abandoned any thoughts it might have had for raising a regular army. From the Union and Confederate governments' point of view, the main requirement in 1861 was to raise men quickly. Accepting locally and privately raised volunteer units met those needs much more rapidly and at less expense than recruiting regular troops. In the summer of 1861 the problem was not for authorities to obtain men but to hold volunteers to manageable numbers. With the benefit of hindsight, both governments should have constituted as a national reserve the hordes of men who were eager to serve. Instead thousands of men went home disappointed. By the spring of 1862 many of these same men were no longer so keen to volunteer and the number of new recruits had become a trickle.

In these circumstances Davis decided he had no option but to introduce a national draft. The Confederacy introduced its first Conscription Law in March 1862. Every white male aged 18 to 35 (soon raised to 45 and later to 50) was now liable for military service and the Law also extended the length of service of those already in the army to the duration of the war. Conscription was tremendously unpopular in the Confederacy: its opponents denounced it as tyrannical. Nevertheless, it did succeed in increasing the Confederate army.

In the North most states adopted a carrot and stick approach. The carrot was bounties - large (and variable) sums of money offered to men who enlisted. The stick, at first, was the Militia Law, enacted by Congress in July 1862. This Law empowered Lincoln to call state militias into Federal service for a period of up to nine months, a power Lincoln was happy to use. Most states managed to enrol enough men but some did have to introduce a militia draft to fill their quotas. In March 1863 the Union finally adopted a system of conscription for all able-bodied men aged 20 to 45. As in the Confederacy, the Conscription Act was bitterly criticised. The fact that it was possible for rich men to avoid the draft by hiring a substitute or paying $300 (for working men half a year's wages for most) was particularly unpopular.

On paper, conscription does not seem to have been very successful in either the North or the South. Under 10 per cent of the troops who fought in the Civil War were actually conscripted. But this statistic does not reflect the full effect of the Conscription Laws. In both North and South, the threat of being drafted was often enough to induce men to volunteer for military service. The fact that conscripts were treated with open contempt by veteran soldiers and had no choice in which regiment they would serve also encouraged men to volunteer. While both governments had difficulties efficiently administering conscription, they did manage to enlist massive armies. By 1865 some 900,000 men had fought for the Confederacy: the Union enlisted about 2,100,000 men.

3 Strategy and Tactics

Improvements in military technology were to change the nature of warfare. In previous wars the smoothbore musket, which had an effective range of less than 100 yards, had been the main infantry weapon. Only the employment of massed volley fire could compensate for its lack of accuracy. Soldiers, therefore, had stood or advanced in close-order formation, either in line or in column. Given the range and inaccuracy of the smoothbore musket, mass infantry charges could often overwhelm an enemy defensive position, as American troops had shown time and again in the Mexican War.

However, in 1855 the smoothbore musket had been supplanted technologically by the rifle-musket. Rifling itself was not new, but loading rifled weapons prior to 1855 was a slow process. With the adoption of the minie ball, an inch-long slug which expanded into the barrel's rifled groove, the rifle-musket could be loaded and fired as fast as the smoothbore musket. Rifle-muskets were still muzzle-loading and single-shot (skilled men, with a clean rifle-musket could fire three shots a minute) but the vital fact was that they were accurate at up to 600 yards and could kill at 1,000 yards. This increased range and accuracy was - ultimately - to have massive effects on the battlefield. But the production of the weapon had been so limited that not until 1863 did nearly all the infantry on both sides have rifle-muskets. The Confederacy relied mainly on European models, especially the British-produced Enfield rifle. The North mass-produced the Spring-field rifle. By 1864 the North was producing breech-loading repeating rifles. However they had a shorter range than the single-fire rifle and were prone to malfunction. Repeating rifles were used mainly by cavalry units rather than by infantry.

In 1861-2, with smoothbore muskets still the norm, troops tended to

A dead Confederate soldier, May 1864

attack in mass formations, with officers usually leading from the front. The defender stood in line formation ready to return volleys. But once the rifle-musket became commonplace battle tactics very much favoured the defending force, which could now fire several rounds at the attacking enemy. Attackers were often shot to pieces before they could get close enough to thrust bayonets. Indeed bayonets soon became redundant: in hand-to-hand combat revolvers, spades or the butt-ends of muskets were better weapons. Less than 1 per cent of battle-wounds in the Civil War were caused by bayonets: 90 per cent of wounds were caused by bullets.

Infantry attacks were even more likely to fail if the defenders had dug trenches or were protected by breastworks. Soldiers quickly learned to use axes and spades to dig in - with amazing speed - and thus improve their safety. By 1864 virtually every position was entrenched, even if it was to be held only for a few hours. The general view was that a three to one superiority was needed to carry trenches defended by good troops.

Most Civil War generals understood the immense power of defence. Given that frontal assaults tended to result in appalling casualties, commanders usually attempted tactical turning movements, sending part of their force to stealthily move to the flank or the rear of the enemy. The defenders' response was usually to keep the flanks so well guarded that the enemy's turning movement was ineffective. Frontal charges, therefore, often became inevitable if there was to be any battle at all. The attacking army stood a reasonable chance of success if it achieved surprise. Given that much of the South was heavily forested, there were often opportunities for an army to sneak up on its opponents as the Confederates did at Shiloh in 1862 and again at Chancellorsville in 1863. Achieving complete surprise normally lay beyond the skill or luck of most generals but even partial surprise could achieve effective results.

In large-scale battles attacking infantry usually approached the enemy in one, two or three lines, of two ranks each, in close order, perhaps a thousand men long. The second line followed about 250 yards behind the first. The third line was often held in reserve for rapid movement to a point of opportunity or danger. Both defenders and attackers usually sent out skirmishes to disconcert or delay the enemy before the main battle occurred. There were few dashing bayonet charges. Instead the attack usually broke down into an 'advance by rushes', elements of the first line working forward, from one bit of cover to the next, with pauses to build up sufficient fire to cover the next rush. If the first line stalled, the second line would be fed in to restore the attack's momentum, followed, if necessary by the third line. The assaulting force, at the moment of collision with the enemy, would thus usually consist of one disordered mass with units badly intermixed. At this stage in proceedings it was virtually impossible for officers to retain control and thus hard to follow up any success that might be achieved, particularly as the bravest men had often been the first to die.

Big battles usually disintegrated into a series of engagements during which infantry traded volleys, charged and counter-charged, with soldiers only vaguely aware of what was happening around them. The majority of battles were hammering matches, not because of the stupidity of the commanders, but simply because of the nature of the combat. In May 1864 some 19,000,000 bullets were fired in a single week of combat in North Virginia. Both sides, and especially the attacker, invariably sustained heavy losses. This made it difficult for the successful army to follow up its victory and win decisively. Usually the beaten army retreated a few miles to lick its wounds; the winners stayed in place to lick theirs. Politicians on both sides denounced their generals as timorous fools for not pursuing a beaten foe. But the politicians did not understand how difficult it was for a victorious army to gather supply trains and exhausted soldiers for a new attack. Moreover, a retreating force usually moved faster than its pursuer, if only because it could hinder pursuit by destroying bridges and cutting down trees to block roads. The only cases of entire armies actually surrendering during the war arose from captured garrisons. There was really only one climactic battle - that at Nashville in December 1864 - which resulted in the destruction of an army - in this case the Confederate one.

Officers, who were expected to lead from the front and by example, suffered far greater casualties than the enlisted men. They were often singled out as targets, in order to disrupt command. Most generals, desiring to share the danger with their men, exposed themselves recklessly to enemy fire. The Union General Sedgewick, for example, in May 1864, refused to take cover in an effort to reassure his men who were unnerved by Confederate sharpshooters. 'They couldn't hit an elephant at this distance,' were his last words before being shot dead by an enemy bullet. Generals stood a 50 per cent greater chance of becoming a casualty than did the ordinary soldier. The Victorian cult of manliness was thus carried to an often counter-productive extreme.

The accuracy of the rifle meant that cavalry were no longer a major force on the battlefield. Cavalry charges against unbroken infantry were usually suicidal. The main role of cavalry was now to scout, make raids against supply lines, guard an army's flanks, screen its movements, obtain supplies, cover retreats, and (very occasionally) to chase a broken enemy. In battle cavalrymen usually dismounted and fought as infantry rather than charging with sabres. The only large-scale cavalry battle of the war, involving some 10,000 men, was at Brandy Station in 1863.

At the start of the war Confederate cavalry proved themselves superior to those of the Union - and this despite the fact that Southern cavalrymen had to provide their own mounts. This superiority was partly the result of good morale and excellent leaders like Jeb Stuart and Nathan Bedford Forrest. But Confederate superiority was also helped by the fact that cavalry units were organised into one autonomous unit, rather than being attached piecemeal to infantry regiments as was the case in the Union army until 1863. Throughout the war Confederate cavalry were admired for their ability to strike quickly and deeply into Northern territory and against Northern supply lines. However, by 1863 Union cavalry were certainly as good as Confederate cavalry and thereafter probably better as men grew in confidence, were better armed (with repeating rifles) and had better horses. (By 1864 the Confederacy had lost its best horse-rearing areas.)

In 1861 artillery was regarded as crucial to battlefield success. Light artillery had proved itself again and again in the Mexican War, with horse batteries galloping to within a few hundred yards of the enemy and pouring a devastating volume of fire - solid shot, grape shot, shell and cannister - into the enemy ranks. However, given the range and accuracy of the rifle-musket, those working the guns were now far more vulnerable to infantry fire. As a result artillerymen were forced to retire to safer, but less effective ranges. Artillery batteries generally had limited effectiveness against an entrenched enemy. Moreover, the terrain over which much of the war was to be fought did not help the artillery. Rugged country and extensive forests made mobility difficult and ensured that few battlefields offered large areas of open ground where guns could be used to maximum effect. Union armies almost always had greater artillery strength than Confederate armies. The North had the manufacturing potential to produce more - and better - guns. In 1861 almost all the artillery batteries were armed with smoothbore guns. Rifled artillery guns, which had a longer range, were introduced as the war progressed. The Confederate artillery possessed a patchwork of widely different guns. Some were purchased abroad. Others were captured from Union armies. The Confederacy did manufacture some of its own guns but these were usually inferior to Union cannon. For all their courage and skill, Confederate artillerymen were continually outmatched by Northern gunners.

4 Communications

Civil War strategy and tactics were considerably affected by improvements in communication. The Civil War was the first great railway war. Both sides were to make use of railways to move masses of men to the front and to keep them supplied. Although railway lines were hard to defend and rails could easily be torn up, they could just as easily be repaired - at least on the Union side. The Confederacy found it increasingly difficult to maintain its railway system and thus optimise its lines of interior communication.

On the Mississippi and its major tributaries, steamboats were to play a vital role in terms of both combat and supply. One ordinary river steamboat could, in one trip, carry enough supplies to support an army of 40,000 men and 18,000 horses for two days.

The telegraph played a key role, enabling commanders to

communicate directly with units on widely separated fronts, thus ensuring co-ordinated advances and/or rapid concentration. The North also made use of observation balloons, especially in the fighting around Richmond in 1862. Balloon surveillance provided useful information and forced the Confederates to maintain elaborate concealment measures.

Both sides set up elaborate intelligence units, which made significant contributions to the Union and Confederate war efforts. Allan Pinkerton ran the Federal Secret Service (not very effectively) until 1862. The Bureau of Military Information, set up in the spring of 1863 was much more efficient. Union sympathisers in the South and runaway slaves often provided useful information. The Confederacy had a variety of espionage and information-gathering agencies operating at different times and in different places. By 1864 its spy network extended as far north as Canada. Women agents, such as Catherine Baxley and Belle Boyd, did particularly good work for the Confederacy.

5 The War's Main Theatres

The Civil War was fought mainly in the Confederacy. There were three main war theatres: North Virginia, the West, and the Trans-Mississippi West.

Both Lincoln and Davis - and many historians since - regarded the fighting in North Virginia as crucial to the outcome of the war. In this area, a flat coastal strip gave way initially to rolling hills and then to the Appalachian Mountains. Richmond, the Confederate capital, lay on the coastal plain. As the crow flies it was only a hundred miles or so from Washington and was the principal target of Union forces. From 1861 onwards the area north - and south - of Richmond was to be the scene of bitter fighting. It was here that Robert E. Lee and 'Stonewall' Jackson were to make their reputations. The fighting area between the mountains and the sea was relatively small. Geographical factors - dense forests, swampy areas and a half-dozen major rivers running west to east - very much favoured the defender.

Beyond the Appalachians lay a vast region of plains and hills stretching to the Mississippi river. The area, extending from Kentucky and Tennessee in the north to the Gulf Coast in the south, was rich agriculturally and in mineral wealth. Given its sheer size and the fact that there were few natural lines of defence, the West was the Confederacy's 'soft underbelly'. The main rivers - the Tennessee, Cumberland and Mississippi - flowed into the heart of the Confederacy and thus could be used for supply purposes by Union forces advancing southwards. The Union's greatest strategical objective at the start of the war was control of the Mississippi which would divide the Confederacy in two.

Both sides had difficulty organising their forces in the West. One problem was simply that of assigning command. Confederate armies

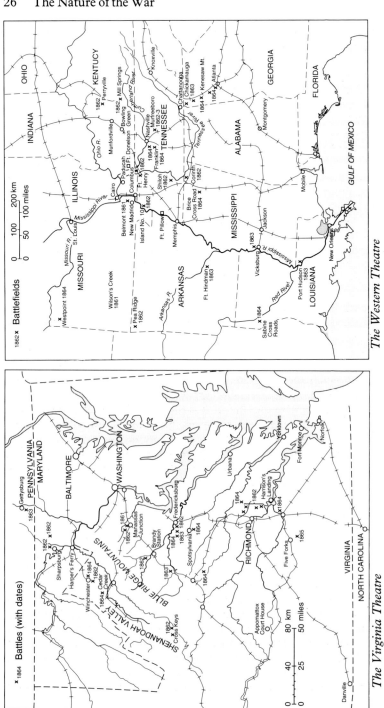

The Western Theatre

The Virginia Theatre

were split into various departments, commanded by different generals. But these generals often found it hard to co-ordinate strategy or even to co-operate. Indeed the Confederate Western commanders devoted almost as much time and energy to quarrelling among themselves as they did to fighting the enemy. Advancing Union forces, on the other hand, had to hold down the areas they occupied and also guard their extensive supply lines. Supply was a major problem for both sides. The Confederate Western armies, usually attempting to do too much over too large an area, were often woefully short of everything.

West of the Mississippi was a massive, but thinly populated area. The fighting here was relatively small scale: none of the numerous minor campaigns had a major effect on the war's outcome. Federal efforts at penetration were few and the Confederate army of the Trans-Mississippi saw major action in two campaigns, both in 1864. In the Trans-Mississippi area the Confederacy had the support of Native Americans - the Choctaws, Chickasaws, Creeks, Seminoles and Cherokees (the so-called Five Civilised Tribes - some of which had black slaves!). The Union also had some Indian support. Plains Indians used the Civil War as an opportunity to wage a defensive war against encroaching white settlers.

There was also a guerilla dimension to the war, especially in Missouri, Kentucky, Arkansas and Tennessee. Few records exist for the Confederate guerilla units because their members were often never formally enrolled, nor were their officers officially commissioned. Men gathered when the call went out, engaged in an operation, and then returned to homes and hideouts until needed again. The men who led such units did so because of their natural ability or because of their community standing. Among the most (in)famous were William Clarke Quantrill and William Anderson. Rarely commanding more than a hundred men at a time, Quantrill and Anderson preyed on Union outposts, patrols, trains and civilian sympathisers, obeying Confederate army orders only as it suited them.

6 The Naval War

From 1861 it was clear that the Northern navy would have a decisive role to play. As soon as the war began the North bought and chartered scores of merchant ships, armed them, and sent them to do blockade duty. By the end of 1861 the Union navy had over 260 warships on duty and 100 more were under construction. Much of this great expansion was due to the dynamism of Secretary of the Navy Gideon Welles and Assistant Secretary Gustavus Fox. They were helped by several factors: first most naval officers remained loyal to the Union; second the North had a proud naval tradition; and third the North had the industrial capacity to build a colossal fleet.

Blockading the Confederacy was a vital function. If the Confederacy was able to sell its cotton in Europe and purchase weapons and manufactured goods in return, the war might continue indefinitely. Given the 3,500 miles of Confederate coastline, the blockade was easier to declare than to enforce. But as the months went by the blockade grew tighter. Although never totally watertight, the blockade undoubtedly hindered the Confederacy's war effort.

The Union navy was also able to use its naval supremacy to transport its troops for major strategical purposes and to strike at Confederate coastal targets. On occasions the navy achieved success without much assistance from the army. In April 1862 New Orleans, the Confederacy's largest town, was brilliantly captured by 60-year-old Admiral David Farragut. (He sailed past two forts and destroyed more than a dozen Confederate vessels.) Loss of many of its major coastal towns weakened the Confederacy and depressed Southern morale.

Just as important as naval supremacy at sea was control of the major Western rivers. River gunboats played a particularly crucial role in 1862 in helping Union troops capture a number of key Confederate fortresses such as Fort Henry and Island No 10. In June 1862 Northern vessels blasted their way through a Confederate river fleet and captured Memphis. By August 1862 Union gunboats operating from New Orleans in the South and others accompanying Union forces advancing from the North, controlled all of the Mississippi except a 150-mile stretch from Vicksburg to Port Hudson. Northern gunboats finally helped to capture both these towns in July 1863. Without the support of the 'inland navy', the Union could not have established or maintained control in the West.

The Confederacy started the war with a dearth of men and ships, little in the way of a naval tradition and few facilities for building a navy. But the Confederacy did have one important human resource - over 300 officers who resigned from the old navy to fight for the Confederacy. Perhaps the most important single individual was the Secretary of the Confederate Navy Stephen Mallory. Mallory, given the unenviable job of creating a navy from scratch, appreciated that the Confederacy could never outbuild the Union: its only hope was the bold adoption of new weapons and methods to outmanoeuvre Northern power. Mallory, aware of British and French experiments with ironclad warships, believed that the best chance to break the Union blockade was for the Confederacy to build or buy several of these revolutionary vessels. In the summer of 1861 he ordered the conversion of the 'Merrimack' (a scuttled Union frigate which the Confederacy had managed to raise) into an ironclad and contracted for the building of two ironclads in New Orleans and two in Memphis.

The Confederacy's greatest moment in the naval war came on 8 March 1862 when the 'Merrimack' (now renamed the 'Virginia' and with its sides sheathed with iron plate) succeeded in sinking two blockading ships in the Hampton Roads. For one day it seemed as though the Confederate navy ruled the waves. Unfortunately for Mallory, whatever the Confederacy could do, the Union could do better. By March 1862 the Union, aware of developments in the South, had its own, oddly-shaped ironclad, the 'Monitor', designed and built by the naval engineer John Ericcson. On 9 March 1862 the first ironclad encounter in history occurred. The battle proved inconclusive. Neither the 'Virginia' nor the 'Monitor' was able to sink the other: there were not even any casualties. But the 'Virginia' was so damaged it was forced to return to port and was soon abandoned by the Confederacy.

Although the South might win a head start, it could scarcely retain a monopoly of new naval weapons. The South had to stretch its resources to build one ironclad: the North was able to mass produce them. Even at its height the Confederate navy never had more than 40 vessels in service. Given its lack of shipbuilding resources, it perhaps did well to build as many warships as it did. Confederate ironclads played a useful role in defending Southern ports but apart from the 'Virginia' never succeeded in attacking and inflicting damage on the enemy. After 1862 it would have been suicidal for them to have sailed out of port: there were just too many Northern ships. There were similar problems on the Western rivers. Although the Confederacy took into service a variety of craft, most were no match for the heavily armed and armoured Union squadrons.

Torpedoes (underwater mines) proved to be the most successful Confederate naval weapon. More than 40 ships were sunk or severely damaged by Confederate torpedoes during the war. The Confederates also produced a mine-carrying submarine - the 'H.L. Hunley'. This succeeded in sinking a Union vessel in 1864 but then went down (or rather never came back up!) with all hands lost.

In 1861 James Bullock was sent to Britain to purchase ships for the Confederacy. A man of business skill and naval knowledge, Bullock managed to evade British neutrality laws and purchase a number of fast raiders such as the 'Alabama' and the 'Florida'. These raiders proceeded to inflict serious damage on Union merchant ships, sinking or capturing some 200 during the course of the war. Although the raiders never seriously threatened Union commerce, their exploits helped Southern morale. Many saw their hit and run tactics as romantic and glorious. The reality, however, was more prosaic. Many of the raiders' crews were foreign-born: they fought on the Confederate side simply because of the prospect of good prize money. Unable to find safe ports for resupply and refitting, the commune raiders eventually found themselves hunted down and either captured or destroyed.

7 A Modern War?

The Civil War reflected the impact of industrial growth. Factories and machines, with their capacity to produce great amounts of arms, ammunition and equipment, transformed and complicated warfare. Outproducing was as important as outmanoeuvring and outfighting the enemy. Given the industrial dimension, railways, the telegraph, mass armies, and the new strategy and tactics which resulted from the effectiveness of the rifle-musket on land, and iron, steam-driven ships on water, many historians consider the Civil War to be the first 'modern' war, more akin to the First World War than the Napoleonic Wars.

However, it is possible to exaggerate the 'moderness' of the Civil War. Although large numbers of men enlisted, there was no battle in the entire war when there was more than 100,000 men on each side. The strategy and tactics of the armies would have been familiar to Napoleon (just as Nelson would have felt at home in most of the ships). During the war there was less technological innovation than is sometimes claimed. Horse-drawn transport and mounted despatch riders remained the norm. Experiments with machine guns, submarines and underwater mines were rudimentary and made little impact on the war's outcome.

Interestingly there was little of the ruthlessness and cruelty that has characterised twentieth-century wars. The scorched-earth policy, adopted by Union Generals Sherman and Sheridan in 1864, was designed to damage property - not kill. Atrocities did occur. Black prisoners of war, for example, were occasionally massacred by Confederates. But such events were notable because of their rarity. Both sides applied the same relatively 'civilised' standards of conduct. On the whole civilians were safe. Women were rarely, if ever, raped. There was a great deal of fraternising between soldiers and civilians of both sides.

In chronological terms, the Civil War came halfway between the Napoleonic Wars and the First World War. Not surprisingly it showed features of both. Its first two years have a Napoleonic feel: its last two years a more twentieth-century feel.

8 Medical Care

Medical facilities were better than in the Napoleonic period and far fewer soldiers died of disease. Nevertheless, by twentieth-century standards, disease mortality was terribly high. The most serious diseases were dysentery, typhoid, pneumonia, malaria, mumps, smallpox, measles, and diphtheria. Epidemics could put whole regiments out of action and disrupt military operations. Although neither side had adequate medical facilities in 1861, this was generally put right as the war progressed. Both sides quickly constructed a network of hospitals of astonishing size (the Confederate Chimborazo Hospital was able to cope with 8,000 patients) and commendable efficiency. Soon over 3,200 women were working as nurses. (Previously army nursing had been an all-male concern.) Female nurses such as Dorothea Dix, Clara Barton and Sally Tompkins deservedly won great reputations, akin to Florence Nightingale in the Crimean War. The US Sanitary Commission, in particular, did splendid work in voluntary nursing and improving sanitary arrangements in Northern camps. Various relief societies in the South did a similar but less well-co-ordinated job. Trained ambulance corps were also established to give first aid on the battlefield and remove the wounded to dressing stations and field hospitals.

The main problem was the state of knowledge of medicine and public health, rather than lack of competence on the part of army doctors and nurses or commitment on the part of governments. Doctors were still working in the 'medical Middle Ages': the revolutionary developments which were to transform medicine came a decade or so later. Treatment of disease, therefore, was partly guesswork. Some drugs worked (e.g. quinine for malaria): some were harmful. Surgeons' skills, especially in amputation, improved with practice but gangrene was a constant problem. Although chloroform now helped men undergoing amputation and serious surgery, there was little awareness of the importance of antiseptics so many men died as a result of basic operations. Wounds to the head, neck, chest and abdomen were usually fatal. The result was that the Civil War soldier was eight times more likely to die of a wound and ten times more likely to die of disease than an American soldier in the First World War. In the Union army 67,000 men were killed in action, 43,000 died of wounds and 224,000 died of disease. (24,000 died from unknown - or other - causes.) Confederate statistics (which are less accurate) indicate a comparable situation.

9 The Soldiers' Experience

The Civil War was very much a people's war. Politicians did their best to direct the struggle. Generals did their best to conduct its campaigns. Yet the real load of fighting, suffering and dying was borne by the ordinary soldiers, the vast majority of whom were civilians-in-arms.

There were some differences between Union and Confederate soldiers. Although the Union army was mainly composed of white native-born Americans, some 20 per cent of its troops had been born overseas, mainly in Ireland, Germany, Britain or Scandinavia. By 1865 10 per cent of Union troops were African Americans. In contrast, 95 per cent of Confederate soldiers were native-born Southerners. Although blacks did many essential non-combat duties, the Confederate army had no black troops until the last days of the war.

According to Bell Wiley (the author of two excellent books, *The Life of Johnny Reb* and *The Life of Billy Yank*), Northern soldiers were slightly better educated than the Confederates: 90 per cent of white Union troops could read and write compared with 80 per cent of Confederates. Southern armies tended to be more rural in composition: some 70 per cent of Southern troops had been farmers compared with only 50 per cent of Union troops. Southern soldiers, Wiley thought, had a more romantic view of the war: Northern troops were more concerned with practicalities - like wages. 'Johnny Reb', again in Wiley's view, was more religious than 'Billy Yank'. Southern troops were reputed to be more independent, proud and less likely to take military discipline seriously. They were almost certainly less well-equipped. But Wiley was convinced that these differences between Johnny Reb and Billy Yank were marginal and were far outweighed by the similarities.

Wiley, who examined thousands of soldiers' letters, was left with the impression that most soldiers had little idea of what exactly they were fighting for. The historian Reid Mitchell reached a similar conclusion: 'American soldiers of the 1860s appear to have been about as little concerned with ideological issues as were those of the 1940s'. In Mitchell's view, the soldiers 'may well have fought during the Civil War for reasons having less to do with ideology than with masculine identity'. Certainly solidarity with one's comrades was - and is - an important motivator in combat. Many men fought bravely not for a cause but simply because they did not want to let their close comrades - and themselves - down.

However, James McPherson has recently examined a cross-section of letters and reached a different conclusion from Wiley and Mitchell. He claims that his letter sample shows that large numbers of men on both sides were intensely aware of the issues at stake and passionately concerned about them. The soldiers, he points out, came from the world's most politicised and democratic society. Southerners believed that they were defending hearth and home against an invading, barbarous army and saw the conflict as the second War for American Independence. Northerners, on the other hand, saw themselves as patriots fighting to save the Union and preserve the great experiment. Men on both sides, therefore, were motivated by simple but very strong

Confederate soldiers captured at Gettysburg in July 1863

patriotism. As casualties mounted many soldiers lost their initial enthusiasm. Some of the men who joined after 1862, especially the conscripts, never had much enthusiasm or idealism. As the conflict wore on desire for revenge on the enemy often became the consuming passion of soldiers on both sides. Nevertheless, in McPherson's view, many soldiers' idealism persisted to the end. General U.S. Grant was of the same view: 'Our armies were composed of men who were able to read, men who knew what they were fighting for'.

Military units usually consisted of men who came from the same neighbourhoods. This was important. Sharing the experience of change from civilian to army life with friends, neighbours and relations, made the transition easier. The closeness of the soldiers to their home community was a powerful impetus for military service. Soldiers feared letting down their family, friends and neighbours. They were aware that any cowardice or misdoing was reported home. So too was bravery, which earned a soldier respect both in his community and in his company. Ethnic affinity was also important. Most of the tens of thousands of Irish, German and Scandinavian troops in the Union army fought in their own regiments, as did black soldiers.

The average age of soldiers in both armies was 25. Although 80 per cent of the men were between 18 and 30 years old, the age spectrum was wide. Drummer boys as young as 9 signed on (the youngest boy killed in battle was 12) and there were also some soldiers over 60. The average soldier was five foot eight and a half inches tall and weighed 143 pounds. Those responsible for recruitment rarely bothered about a potential soldiers' age, health or fitness. Physical examinations of recruits in the early stages of the war were a sham. This accounts for the fact that scores of women succeeded in passing as men and entering the armies.

Following enlistment and muster into an official unit, recruits underwent basic training. This involved learning the rudiments of camp life, marching, weapon training, and drilling. Drilling often took up hours of a soldier's day. The goal of drill was to move disciplined manpower quickly and effectively into position on the battlefield to deliver the maximum firepower at the enemy. Men had to be trained to follow orders so automatically that even amid the fear and frenzy of battle they would respond to orders and act as part of a cohesive unit. (Many of the commands were given by bugle or drum, since a voice did not carry far in battle.) Soldiers in cavalry and artillery units had to perfect their own distinctive drill and weapon training.

By European (but not American) standards, Union soldiers were well paid. In 1861 they received $11 a month but this was raised to $13 and then to $16. Inflation resulted in a depreciation in purchasing power, but many Union soldiers were still able to send money home. Confederate soldiers were supposed to receive $11 a month but payment was a haphazard thing at best and hyper-inflation in the South meant that the money was almost worthless. Most Southerners, therefore, effectively fought without pay.

Northern soldiers were better equipped than the 'rebels'. By 1862 most Union infantry soldiers wore a standard blue uniform which comprised cap, jacket, trousers and heavy shoes. Confederate soldiers wore more assorted colours. Some wore grey - in many different shades. Others wore clothes they had stripped from the bodies of the Union dead and often dyed 'butternut' - a yellowish-brown colour. Recent research suggests that most Confederate infantrymen, contrary to popular myth, were reasonably well supplied with clothing, if not smart uniforms. But boots and shoes were a major problem, the Confederacy being short of both leather and skilled shoe-makers.

The common soldier carried on his back nearly everything he would need to fight the enemy and survive the elements. The assorted gear of a fully equipped infantryman might weigh as much as 50 lbs. To lighten the load, soldiers on campaign often discarded what they regarded as excess items, especially overcoats. But at the very least a soldier had to carry a rifle with bayonet, a cartridge box, a haversack, a cape, a blanket, and a canteen. Many also carried a razor, towel, soap, comb, knife, writing implement, Bible, family portraits, an oil-cloth groundsheet that doubled up as a tent floor and as a poncho, socks, money, sewing kit, tobacco pouch, matches, a pipe, eating utensils and a cup.

Union soldiers were usually far better fed than Confederates. Indeed, the only criticism that British observers could make of the standard of the Union army ration was that there was too much of it! Although soldiers received generous quantities, army food - which mainly comprised salted meat and hard tack - was dull, often vermin-ridden and not particularly nutritious. Supply problems meant that Southern troops frequently had to scavenge for whatever they could get and hunger was a constant companion.

For most men the novelty of army life was short-lived. In its place came homesickness, hard labour and sheer tedium. Most resented the constant drill and irksome discipline. There was much else that was unpleasant. In summer soldiers suffered from heat and from the fact that they were constantly on the move. While they had more time to establish more permanent accommodation during the winter months, tents, log huts and makeshift shanties were often poor protection from the weather. Inattention to latrine procedures and garbage pits meant that there was usually an overbearing stench. Fleas and lice were an additional nastiness.

In camp - and on the march - there was a constant search for diversions to overcome the tedium of army routine. One of the most popular passtimes was letter-writing to loved ones back home. Music played an important role in sustaining morale. Robert E. Lee went so far as to say: 'I don't believe we can have an army without music'. Regimental bands welcomed recruits, provided entertainment in camp and inspired the troops both on the march and in battle. Individual soldiers sometimes carried a banjo or a fiddle. Each side had its own favourite songs and tunes: 'Battle Cry of Freedom' and 'John Brown's Body' - which had many different, often vulgar, variations - were popular with the Union army: Confederate soldiers liked 'Dixie' and the 'Bonnie Blue Flag'. Soldiers of both armies liked sentimental songs such as 'Home Sweet Home'. Sports - boxing, wrestling, running, jumping, and the new game of baseball - were popular with men often gambling on the results. Many soldiers would gamble on anything - but especially cards and dice. There was relatively little drunkenness. While there was considerable pillaging, crimes against persons were rare. Soldiers often frequented brothels when they were on leave (especially in Washington where there were 450 bordellos). Furloughs, however, were seldom granted. Union troops were often stationed too far from home to get much use from a furlough while Confederate troops were too few and too badly needed to be allowed generous leaves.

Some soldiers took their own leave. One in seven Confederate soldiers and one in ten Union troops eventually deserted. They did so for a variety of reasons: boredom; fear; concern for families at home; poor food; and often simple lack of commitment. The fact that the odds were in favour of the escape attempt being successful also encouraged desertion. Authorities did their best to lure deserters back into the ranks with periodic pardon proclamations and general amnesties. There was little consistency in the punishment meted out to those deserters who were caught. Some were dishonourably discharged; others were sentenced to hard labour; a few were shot or hung.

Actual fighting took up only a very small part of a soldier's time. The campaign season was usually in the spring or summer and men often marched for weeks without encountering the enemy. But battle was often at the forefront of men's minds. They knew it was the ultimate test. Battles like Antietam and Gettysburg resulted in death on a scale that Americans had never seen before. Most men, initially shocked by the thick smoke, crash of musketry and cannonfire, the shouts and screams of the living and dying, fought well - usually with little idea of what was happening around them. Real bravery was needed to charge across open ground against entrenched positions. Amazingly, men in the early part of the war often begged for the privilege of carrying their regiment's colours in front of the ranks, knowing full well that in battle colour bearers were usually among the first to die. (By 1863, as men realised that courage was often more futile than sublime, it became increasingly difficult to get men to carry the colours!) Most men seem to have been motivated in battle by concepts of duty and honour. Many were prepared to die for their respective causes and countries. The most prevalent fear expressed in letters was not so much that of being killed or wounded but of displaying cowardice that would bring humiliation to themselves and their families.

Death by disease was actually far more likely than death in battle.

Ironically, the supposedly unsoldierly easterners from the towns were far less likely to die of disease than westerners, many of whom came from isolated farms and who had been unexposed to childhood diseases like measles and mumps. The major killers - dysentery, typhoid fever, pneumonia and malaria - were triggered by impure water, poor food, exposure to rain, cold and heat, insects, and general filth.

Soldiers also faced the prospect of capture. Neither side in 1861 had made any provision for taking large numbers of prisoners. Technically, all the Confederate prisoners were traitors and could have faced the death penalty. Lincoln, aware that this would simply have led to terrible Southern reprisals, condoned prisoner exchange or parole in the first two years of the war. But in 1863 the Union suspended further exchange of prisoners, technically on the grounds of Confederate violations of agreements, but actually because the South (with its smaller population) had more to gain from exchanges than the North. The fact that the Confederacy was unwilling to accept that captured black Northern soldiers should be treated as legitimate prisoners-of-war was a further problem. Both sides in 1863-4, therefore, suddenly had to deal with thousands of captives. Warehouses, school buildings, even open fields, were commandeered as prison camps. Most were terribly overcrowded and prisoners had inadequate food, shelter, clothing and medical services. The result was a shockingly high mortality rate. Union prisoners particularly suffered. This was more accident than intent. By 1864 the Confederacy was having difficulty feeding its own soldiers and people, never mind captured Yankees. The most notorious Confederate prison camp was Andersonville in Georgia, which by the summer of 1864 had become the fourth biggest 'settlement' within the Confederacy. Each prisoner had a daily ration of one teaspoon of salt, three tablespoons of beans and a half-pint of unsifted cornmeal. The stream (perversely called Sweet Water) which ran through the camp served as the only water supply and as a sewer. Over 25 per cent of the camp's 50,000 inmates died from malnutrition and disease. After the war, Henry Wirtz, the Andersonville camp commandant, was to be the only man executed for war crimes. During the war, 194,743 Northern soldiers were imprisoned. Some 30,128 died. This compares with 214,865 Confederate prisoners, of whom 25,976 died.

Most men, despite the horrors they witnessed and/or experienced, continued to have faith in God. Indeed the war, perhaps because of the ever-present prospect of death, seems to have led to a strengthening of religious conviction. Army chaplains, few in number and variable in quality, were not particularly instrumental in this. For most soldiers Churches distributed prodigious quantities of religious tracts among the troops. The Confederate armies were swept by a great evangelical religious revival from the autumn of 1862 onwards (and particularly over the winter of 1863-4), so much so that for some the war became a crusade. The evangelical fervour of the Southern troops was not paralleled by a similar outbreak of religious enthusiasm within the Confederacy as a whole and nothing like it occurred in the Union army. The South's military setbacks in 1863 - seen by some as punishment inflicted by God - may have contributed to the revivalist spirit. The fact that the bulk of Southern soldiers came from areas where evangelical, 'born again' meetings were relatively common may also help explain the phenomenen. The view that the revivalist fervour resulted from severe stress and shell-shock is not satisfactory, if only because Union soldiers, under similar stress and shock, did not react in the same way.

The following extracts are from letters written by Tally Simpson of the 3rd South Carolina Volunteers during 1862. Simpson was a well-educated and thoughtful man who fought for the Confederacy in all the major engagements in the Virginia theatre from 1861 to 1863. Surprisingly, given that he was well-connected and from a rich family (he took his slave Zion with him to war), he never rose above the rank of corporal. Simpson was obviously not a typical Southern soldier. Nevertheless these extracts from his correspondence do give us a 'feel' of the war.

Custis' Farm on the Peninsula, Va. April 24th 1862

1 Dear Sister
　　… We are still living in the open air without tents, but with little houses made of blankets, we make out very well. I am doing remarkably well with the small amount of clothing I have on hand.
5 I am fearful about keeping myself shod. My boots are giving way, and there are no prospects for another pair … During our idle hours, we pass our times in reading, fishing, and thinking of the women … Zion is in good health and spirits.

Camp Jackson [Va] Wednesday, June 18th 1862

1 Dear Sister
　　… The dull routine of camp life continues daily, and I am becoming entirely disgusted with anything that pertains to this form of life. Drill, drill, drill; work, work, work; and guard, guard,
5 guard. Eat, e-a-t. Alas. Would that we had eating to do in proportion to work and drill. But nothing but bacon and bread, bread and bacon. Occasionally we get cowpeas which I consider a great luxury. We are all doing finely, but I have had a very severe cough for some time which of late has rather frightened me. Zion is well again and sends his love to Hester and his family and begs to be remembered to the white family.

10 Conclusion

The romantic assumptions of 1861 were soon shattered by the terrible reality of war. Army life meant homesickness, irksome discipline, exhausting marches and a few dreadful hours of battle. The casualty rates, both from disease and battle, were dreadfully high: one in five of the soldiers who fought in the Civil War died in it. Yet most soldiers did survive and most afterwards came to look back on the war with both pride and nostalgia. Perhaps there was more reason for the former than the latter. Although the Civil War soldier was rarely a dashing hero, most men were resilient, long-suffering and courageous. The hard school of experience turned the enthusiastic mobs of 1861 into tough soldiers whose powers of endurance and willingness to absorb punishment astounded many European observers.

But there was also some cause for nostalgia. Cheerfulness and high youthful spirits often seem to have outweighed dejection in the Civil War armies. For most men the war was the greatest experience of their lives. They felt they were doing their duty for country, community, family and friends. Although the scale of the battle carnage often hit soldiers hard, people in the mid-nineteenth century were more used to death and suffering than people. Today most soldiers succeeded in adopting an attitude of indifference to the brutalities around them. Many became fatalistic, seeing death as part of God's plan. In retrospect, the war became filled with minor adventures and was memorable for good fellowship and lasting friendship. Few veterans seem to have suffered much trauma. Many seem to have continued to view the war as worthy and heroic.

Making notes on '*The Nature of the War*'

This chapter is designed to give you an overview of the nature of the war. For many years military history was unfashionable with academic historians who preferred to study economic, social and political developments. Indeed several books, purportedly on the Civil War, have totally disregarded military aspects of the conflict. Such an approach is at best unbalanced. Events on the battlefield obviously determined the outcome of the conflict and therefore need to be understood. Chapters 3 and 8 will examine the main military events of the war. Your notes on this chapter should help you understand what the war was like, particularly for the 3,000,000 or so rank-and-file soldiers.

Answering essay questions on '*The Nature of the War*'

It is likely you will use evidence from this chapter to answer specific questions about the nature of the Civil War. Consider the following:

'From 'Johnny Reb' and 'Billy Yanks' point of view, there was
little that was glorious or romantic about the American Civil
War'. Do you agree?

The golden rule for writing history essays is simple: answer the set
question! The first paragraph - or introduction - is often crucial. It is the
first opportunity for you to impress (or depress) an examiner. There is
no perfect way of writing an introduction but there are certain things you
ought to be trying to do. Firstly you should be trying to establish the
precise meaning of the question. This often involves defining the most
important terms in the title. You should also be identifying the key issues
within the question which you will go on to develop. Try to write an
introduction. Good essay answers often contain seven or eight
paragraphs. So now plan seven or eight suitable paragraphs for this
question. Remember that these paragraphs should be designed to
include all the information which you want to bring to bear to a) show
the examiner the depth of your knowledge and b) answer the question
and prove your case.

Another essential part of any essay is the final paragraph or
conclusion. In this you should be drawing together the threads of your
argument and giving your opinion on the central issue in the question
set. Your conclusion should not be loaded down with factual
information. Nor should you spring some new and previously
unexplored idea that you have just thought of on the reader. The
conclusion should stem logically from the rest of the essay. Do not be
afraid to give your view: after all, this is what questions usually ask for.
But try not to use phrases like, 'I think'. A personal view does not sound
very authoritative. It is generally considered better style to write 'the
evidence suggests' or 'it seems likely that'.

Source-based questions on 'The Nature of the War'

1 Visual Images
Examine carefully the photographs on pages 21 and 32. Answer the
following questions:
a) Why do you think there so many portrait photographs of soldiers and
   why so many photographs of dead bodies? (4 marks)
b) What can the two photographs tell us about the Civil War? (5 marks)
c) What do you think are the main limits - and the main problems - of
   Civil War photographic evidence? (6 marks)

2 The Letters of Tally Simpson
Read carefully the extracts from Tally Simpson's letters on pages 37.
Answer the following questions:
a) What seem to have been Tally Simpson's main concerns? (4 marks)
b) To what extent do you think these letters record the typical

experiences and feelings of Southern soldiers in the war? (5 marks)
c) Do you think the tone of Union letters would have been similar or
    different? Explain your answer. (6 marks)

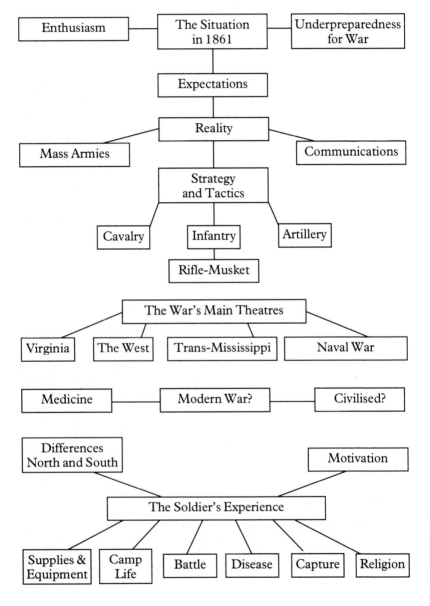

Summary - The Nature of the War

CHAPTER 3

The War 1861-3

1 Introduction

Confident of Northern strength, Abraham Lincoln anticipated a short war. The fact that the war did not end quickly was largely due to events on the battlefield. Confederate forces fought better than most Northerners had expected - and their own forces less well. However, Confederate success was largely confined to northern Virginia. Elsewhere Union forces won a series of important victories. This chapter will examine the main military events. It is perhaps a truism that wars are won and lost on battlefields. But a surprising number of recent books on the Civil War have tended to ignore the military aspects of the war. They do so at their peril. Had a battle or campaign turned out differently, it is possible that the outcome of the war might have been different. Had the North lost battle after battle, Northerners might well have lost the will to continue the struggle. Had Union commanders fought with more skill - and luck - in the years 1861-3 the war might have been over sooner. Ironically, it might well have been in the best interests of - white - Southerners if this had happened and if they had thus fought less well!

2 Northern Plans in 1861

In 1861 Lincoln hoped to quickly suppress what he saw as a domestic insurrection. Winfield Scott, General-in-Chief of the Union army, was less optimistic of winning an easy victory. Like General McDowell, commander of the growing Federal army around Washington, Scott thought it would take many months to train and equip the armies needed to crush the insurrection. Scott, therefore, supported the so-called Anaconda Plan, the aim of which was to put increasing pressure on the Confederacy by naval blockade and by winning control of the Mississippi river. Such a strategy, Scott thought, would deprive the South of military resources, squeeze life out of the Confederacy (thus the name of the 'Anaconda Plan') and bring Southerners to their senses.

But Lincoln and most Northerners looked for a quick decisive blow. Richmond, the Confederate capital, was only 100 miles from Washington. 'Forward to Richmond' soon became the cry in the Northern press. Lincoln accepted that many Union troops were untrained but as he wrote to McDowell: 'You are green, it is true, but they are green; you are all green alike'. As the initial three-month enlistment period was about to run out, Lincoln urged McDowell to march on Richmond.

3 Confederate Plans in 1861

President Davis's first instinct was to wage a guerilla-type war, trading space for time and making the war so costly to the Union that it would accept defeat. But several factors prevented Davis adopting such a strategy. First and foremost, he was pledged to defend every portion of the Confederacy. Lost territory would obviously result in a depletion of resources and might also make it difficult to sustain Southern morale. Davis was also aware of the confident Southern mood: most Southerners believed they could whip any number of Northerners. Davis, therefore, supported the recruitment of conventional armies, hoping to make use of the Confederacy's interior lines of communication which should enable it to concentrate dispersed forces against a Union invasion.

The Confederate high command soon rejected the notion of passive defence, pursuing instead what has become known as 'offensive-defensive' strategy. Although relying essentially on defence, Confederate armies exploited opportunities for counter-attacks and raids. The aim was to prevent the enemy applying fatal pressure in all parts by attacking him at selected points when the opportunity arose. Although some historians have been critical of this strategy, it is hard to imagine a better one. A war fought purely on the defensive was unlikely to bring about Confederate success: it would simply allow the Union to pick off the South almost at will. By occasionally going on the offensive, Confederate armies could cause mayhem to Union plans and might win a dramatic victory which would seriously damage Northern morale.

4 First Manassas

In 1861 both sides saw Virginia as the crucial theatre of war. The main Confederate army of 22,000 men, led by Beauregard, was positioned south of the Bull Run river at Manassas Junction. General Joseph Johnston commanded another army of 11,000 men in the Shenandoah Valley. On the 16 July 1861 General McDowell, urged on by Lincoln and the Northern press, marched south with some 30,000 men. Although McDowell's advance was painfully slow, his attack on 21 July was well conceived and he came near to winning a decisive victory. However, Confederate forces fought bravely, especially Thomas Jackson's brigade which stood 'like a stonewall' (hereafter Jackson became known as 'Stonewall' Jackson): and were saved by the arrival of Johnston's troops, many of whom travelled by rail from the Shenandoah Valley. The Northern attack was held and then, as the Confederates advanced, Union troops panicked and fled back to Washington. The Confederacy had won the first major battle of the war. Southern casualties amounted to 440 dead and 1,600 wounded: the Union army lost over 600 dead, 950 wounded and 1,200 prisoners. The

Confederates, who invariably named battles after the nearest large settlement, called the battle Manassas. Northerners, who usually named battles after the nearest geographical feature, called it Bull Run.

For several days after the battle Washington seemed to be in danger. In the event, however, the Confederacy made no attempt to follow up its victory. Some see this as a missed opportunity to win the war. But in July 1861 the victorious Southern army was as disorganised as the routed Union army: it was desperately short of supplies; and probably in no condition to attack Washington's strong defences. In any case, even if the Confederates had captured Washington, it is unlikely that this would have brought an end to the war.

Victory in the war's first major battle was a mixed blessing for the Confederacy. It may have made some Southerners overconfident and complacent. Defeat, on the other hand, spurred the North on to more determined efforts. But victory did give the Confederates in Virginia an *esprit de corps* - and an edge - reinforced by a further victory at Ball's Bluff in October. Over the winter Johnston maintained the Confederate line near Manassas and along the Potomac river below Washington. There was little fighting. 'All Quiet along the Potomac' was a popular and appropriate song in 1861-2.

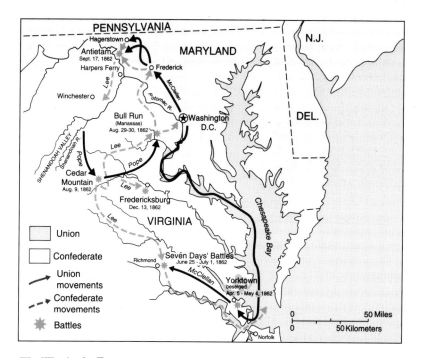

The War in the East

5 General McClellan

After Manassas McDowell was replaced by 34-year-old General George McClellan, who had fought in the Mexican War and been sent as an American observer to the Crimean War. Credited (wrongly!) with some minor victories in West Virginia, McClellan exuded an air of optimism. Within a few months, he had replaced Scott as General-in-Chief and boasted, 'I can do it all'.

McClellan remains one of the most controversial figures of the war. Opinion was divided about him in 1862 and historians still remain divided today. Certainly a case can be made for McClellan. An able administrator, he restored the morale of the army - now called the Army of the Potomac - which soon numbered 150,000 men. There is no doubt that he was popular with the soldiers who referred to him affectionately as 'Little Mac' and the 'Young Napoleon'. McClellan's supporters claim he was a man of considerable strategic vision who was betrayed by Republican political intrigue (McClellan was a Democrat who had no wish to emancipate the slaves) and by poor intelligence (from Allan Pinkerton's information service). As an official American observer of the Crimean War, McClellan appreciated the foolishness of frontal assaults against well-defended positions. Anxious not to alienate Southerners and create scars that might take a generation to heal, his hope of winning the war by manoeuvre and bringing it to an end without too much gore, also made - humane - sense.

But, despite these points, it is easier to attack than to defend McClellan. Even his supporters concede that he was an arrogant egotist, often claiming credit that really belonged to others. He failed to work collaboratively with his political masters, whom he constantly derided. Lincoln (whom he quite liked) was 'nothing more than a well-meaning baboon ... the original gorilla'. The main charge levied against McClellan is that, having built a fine army, he was too reluctant to use it. Indecisive, overcautious and perhaps too much of a perfectionist, his actual military moves were anything but Napoleonic. He had a chronic disposition to exaggerate the odds against him and to overestimate the fighting capacity of the Southern soldier. He accepted Pinkerton's - false - intelligence reports when others did not. (It did not require a genius to realise that the South had fewer men and resources!) His hope of winning the war (and glory) without hard fighting was unrealistic.

Over the winter of 1861-2 McClellan, determined to avoid the kind of premature advance which he felt had brought about defeat at Manassas, refused to move. Although his army was twice the size of the Confederate force facing him, he believed he was outnumbered. Lincoln (who remained loyal to McClellan much longer than most Republicans) and the Northern public grew increasingly impatient - not least the new Secretary of State of War, Edwin Stanton.

In late January 1862 a frustrated Lincoln issued War Order No 1, ordering 'a general movement of Land and Naval forces of the US against insurgent forces to start on February 22'. But McClellan now went down with typhoid fever and was confined to bed for three weeks. On his recovery, rather than lead a direct march on Richmond as Lincoln envisaged, McClellan devised an ambitious flanking attack, making use of the Union's naval dominance. His intention was to ferry the bulk of his army to Urbana so that it was between Richmond and the Confederate army at Manassas. Although Lincoln had some doubts about the plan - he feared it would leave Washington exposed to a Confederate attack - he was anxious to get McClellan moving and sanctioned it. Lincoln wrote to McClellan: 'all I ask is for you to just pitch in'.

Just as McClellan was ready to move, the Confederate army, well aware of his intention, withdrew to new lines south of the Rappahannock river. McClellan had no option but to abandon his Urbana strategy. Typically, he claimed his plan had been a triumph, winning a huge chunk of territory at no cost in lives. But McClellan's critics pointed out that the Confederate defences at Manassas seemed to be relatively weak. Many of their cannon, for example, were so-called 'Quaker guns' - pieces of timber made to look like cannon. A direct Northern attack might well have won the day.

McClellan, still anxious to avoid a frontal attack, now planned to attack Richmond up the peninsula between the York and James rivers. To his dismay, Lincoln insisted on part of the army being left to protect Washington.

6 The Peninsula Campaign

In April 1862 the Army of Potomac, 121,000 strong, was transported to Fortress Monroe - 70 miles from Richmond. 'I have not come here to wage war upon the defenseless, upon non-combatants, upon private property, nor upon the domestic institutions of the land,' announced McClellan. It soon seemed as though he not come to wage war at all. The only Confederate army ready to impede McClellan's advance was a force of 11,000 men at Yorktown commanded by General Magruder. Magruder (who was keen on amateur dramatics) convinced McClellan that he had thousands more men, simply by marching his small force up and down. Instead of attacking, McClellan settled down to a one month siege of Yorktown, giving the Confederates plenty of time to send reinforcements to the peninsula. Just as he was ready to attack Yorktown, the Confederates withdrew. McClellan, delighted that he had won another bloodless victory, advanced cautiously up the peninsula, finally reaching the outskirts of Richmond by late May. His forces outnumbered the Confederates opposing him by two to one, but McClellan, believing that it was he who was outnumbered, awaited reinforcements.

McClellan never got his reinforcements - largely because of Stonewall Jackson's Shenandoah Valley campaign. Jackson, with 18,000 men, was sent into the Valley to ensure that (far larger) Union forces did not move south to Richmond. Jackson, a former regular soldier and - dreadful - teacher at the Virginia Military Institute, was remote and eccentric. A religious fanatic who saw himself as God's instrument (he preferred not to fight on the sabbath), Jackson demanded a great deal of his men, who at first regarded him with great suspicion. However, from March to June 1862 he was to prove himself a brilliant, attack-minded soldier and won the grudging respect of his troops. During that period he fought six battles, marched his 'foot cavalry' hundreds of miles, baffled his opponents, inflicted 7,000 casualties on Union forces, seized huge quantities of supplies, diverted 60,000 Northern soldiers from other tasks, and generally inspired the South. ('He who does not see the hand of God in this is blind, sir, blind,' said Jackson.) Lincoln, worried at the threat which Jackson might pose to Washington, reversed his decision to send forces to help McClellan and instead sent McDowell and 40,000 men to the Shenandoah Valley. It was Jackson, not McDowell, who marched south to participate in the fighting around Richmond.

Despite Jackson's success, the Confederacy seemed to be on the verge of defeat in May 1862. Confederate forces had suffered severe setbacks elsewhere, not least the loss of New Orleans in April 1862. Most of the Mississippi valley was now in Union hands and McClellan seemed certain to capture Richmond. In April 1862 Stanton, anticipating an early victory, called a halt to Federal recruiting. In May, the New York Tribune proclaimed that 'the rebels ... are panic-stricken or despondent. It now requires no very far-reaching prophet to predict the end of this struggle'.

7 Robert E. Lee

On 31 May General Johnston launched an attack on McClellan's forces outside Richmond. The battle of Fair Oaks (or Seven Pines) was hopelessly executed. Poor planning and an almost unbelievable degree of confusion among his subordinates dissipated what Johnston (and historians subsequently) perceived to be a wonderful opportunity to defeat the Army of the Potomac. By the time the battle ended on 1 June 1862, the South had lost 6,000 casualties and the North 5,000. The most important outcome from the Confederacy's point of view was the fact that Johnston was seriously wounded. He was immediately replaced by Robert E. Lee.

Lee, a 55-year-old Virginian and son of a former Revolutionary War general, was related to most of the first families of Virginia. Having served with distinction in the Mexican War, many considered him America's finest soldier in 1861. Lincoln had offered him high command in the Union army but Lee had remained loyal to his state.

The early part of the war had not gone well for him and after some embarrassing setbacks, first in West Virginia and then in South Carolina, he became Davis's chief military adviser.

But now Lee had another opportunity to display his prowess. Renaming his army the 'Army of Northern Virginia', he determined to seize the initiative and end the siege of Richmond. In order to neutralise McClellan's preponderance in numbers, his first priority was to strengthen his defences. Southern soldiers, grumbling about wielding shovels instead of weapons, nicknamed Lee 'King of Spades'. But 'Granny' Lee's plans were anything but timid and irresolute. He aimed to detach a large part of his force, join up with Stonewall Jackson's army and carry out an audacious flanking movement on the Union army.

Lee finally hurled his men against the Federals during the last week of June. The week of battles which followed is known as 'The Seven Days'. Lee struck first at Mechanicsville. Jackson's late arrival meant that little was achieved. On 27 June Lee attacked again at Gaines Mill. Again Jackson failed to perform well and the result was a grinding frontal assault. Despite savage losses, Confederate forces finally surged over the enemy line. Pursuit of the beaten foe proceeded sluggishly from 28-30 June with another poorly co-ordinated bloodbath at Frayser's Farm. In the last major battle of the campaign, at Malvern Hill on 1 July, Lee lost 5,000 men to the Union's 3,000.

In terms of bodycount, Lee's Seven Days offensive was a Confederate disaster. Southern losses amounted to 20,614 men: Union losses were only 15,849. Faulty staff work, overcomplicated battle plans, defects in command structure and poor intelligence led to Lee making a number of disjointed and costly attacks. He was also let down by his subordinates, especially Jackson who was strangely lethargic, repeatedly failing to carry out orders. Lee, who had failed to destroy the Union army, was naturally disappointed with the results of his offensive.

The Seven Days campaign, however, was most certainly a Confederate victory. McClellan, confused and demoralised by events, ended his siege of Richmond and retreated back down the peninsula. In effect he accepted defeat. His excuse was that his forces had been outnumbered. The reality was that he had easily outnumbered Lee.

8 Second Manassas and Antietam

Through July and early August McClellan's army continued to menace Richmond from the south. Meanwhile Lincoln attempted to consolidate Federal forces around Washington into a new Army of Virginia to attack from the north. General John Pope, who had won some small victories in the West, was appointed commander. Another Western soldier, Henry Halleck, was appointed General-in-Chief. Lincoln hoped he would become a vigorous commander, co-ordinating Union strategy. (Instead, he became a high-level adviser - a paper-shuffler - who neither laid down nor enforced a comprehensive strategy for the war as a whole.) McClellan, meanwhile, was ordered to evacuate the peninsula and join Pope's new army. With a united army, Pope would then advance on Richmond.

Lee determined to strike first. After reorganising his army into two corps under Longstreet and Jackson, Lee advanced northwards in mid-August with some 55,000 men. Dividing his army, Lee sent Jackson on a long sweep west and north of Pope, who was still awaiting McClellan's - slow - arrival. Jackson's men, in contrast, marched 54 miles in 36 hours. On August 26-27, Jackson's 25,000 troops captured Pope's main supply depot at Manassas Junction. But Pope, strengthened at last by advanced units of McClellan's army, confidently prepared to attack Jackson's outnumbered force which was dug in at Bull Run. The Second Battle of Bull Run (or Second Manassas), fought on August 29-30, was a Union disaster. Failing to appreciate the obvious - that the rest of the Confederate army was marching to Jackson's assistance - Pope was defeated when Longstreet's corps attacked his left flank. After a brilliantly conceived campaign, the Confederate army had come close to winning the decisive victory that Lee was seeking. But in the event Pope managed to extricate most of his troops and pulled back towards Washington. Pope's poor generalship, however, had cost the Union 16,000 men (Lee lost only 9,000). Reluctantly Lincoln reappointed McClellan as commander-in-chief. 'Again I have been called upon to save the country,' wrote McClellan to his wife.

In early September, Lee, still intent on maintaining the initiative, invaded Maryland with 40,000 men. (Jackson, commanding the rest of the army, was sent to capture the rich stores at Harper's Ferry, which he accomplished in mid-September.) Given that Lee was riding the crest of a military tide of impressive proportions, any other strategic decision would probably have been foolish. Lee's aims were many: to take the fight to the North; feed (and shoe!) his soldiers; protect Virginia's harvest; keep Northern armies away from Richmond; gain Maryland volunteers; threaten Washington but possibly capture Harrisburg; win the elusive decisive victory; demoralise the North; and persuade Britain and France to recognise the Confederacy. Confederate morale, low in May 1862, was now sky high, particularly as another Southern army, led by General Bragg, also invaded Kentucky. After Second Manassas, thought Confederate General Longstreet, 'we had the most brilliant prospects the Confederates ever had'.

Lee's northern invasion, however, did not go to plan. He lost more soldiers by straggling and desertion than he gained from pro-Confederate Marylanders. He also lost a copy of his detailed operational orders which mysteriously fell into McClellan's hands. (The orders were found wrapped around some cigars in an abandoned Confederate camp: Lee later insisted that without the mistake of the lost orders, he would have crushed McClellan.) Aware that Lee's army was divided, McClellan was now in a tremendous position to defeat him. Although he frittered away much of the dazzling advantage presented to him, he did force Lee back toward the Potomac river.

Instead of retreating into Virginia, Lee took up a position east of Sharpsburg, behind Antietam Creek, still hoping to win a decisive victory. Given that he was hopelessly outnumbered, that both his flanks were vulnerable, that he failed to entrench, and that he had the Potomac behind him, Lee's decision to offer battle seems incredible. If McClellan had attacked on 15. or 16 September Lee must surely have been defeated. Fortunately for Lee's reputation, McClellan did not attack.

On 16 September Jackson's corps rejoined Lee's army which reduced the odds. Even so McClellan still had a numerical advantage of two to one when he finally gave battle on 17 September. The battle of Antietam (or Sharpsburg), partly because it was so badly handled by McClellan, was really three separate battles. All three Northern attacks were partly successful but none were followed through to complete success and Lee managed to hang on. Antietam was the bloodiest single day battle of the Civil War. The Confederacy had over 10,000 casualties: the North 14,000 casualties; 12,000 men died - four times the number of Americans who died on D Day in 1944.

Lee's outnumbered Army of Northern Virginia had staged one of its most impressive performances. But McClellan was able to claim a victory because on 18 September Lee finally retreated into Virginia. Indeed, Antietam can be seen as THE turning point of the war. Within days of the battle Lincoln issued his famous Emancipation Proclamation (see page 00). Lee's failure to win a decisive victory meant there was now little likelihood of European intervention. But McClellan failed to follow up his 'victory'. Lincoln, exasperated with McClellan's excuses for inactivity, finally relieved him of command in November, replacing him with General Ambrose Burnside. Lee wrote to his wife: 'I hate to see McClellan go. He and I had grown to understand each other so well'.

9 The War in the West: 1861-2

The war was not confined to Virginia. Just as important was the West - an area the Confederacy found far harder to defend than north Virginia. In 1861 Lincoln divided the Union's western forces: General Halleck was to concentrate on winning control of the Mississippi while General Don Carlos Buell was to drive Confederate forces from Kentucky and Tennessee. Lincoln urged the two commanders to co-operate and hoped for a joint offensive. However, the divided command led to some confusion. Moreover, neither Halleck nor Buell was prepared to risk failure by attacking too soon. Both men had good excuses for delay. Their forces were short of arms, equipment and transport for most of 1861.

Davis sent General Albert Sidney Johnston to command the Confederate forces between the Appalachian and Ozark Mountains. Aware of Davis's intention to defend every foot of Southern territory, Johnston scattered his 40,000 troops along the southern borders of Kentucky and Missouri. His line lacked both naturally defensible terrain and good east-west communications so Federal troops were soon able to menace it at several points. Johnston hoped that a number of forts built at strategic points on the important rivers would hold up any Union advance.

In early 1862 Union armies finally went on the offensive. In January 1862 troops from Buell's army, led by General Thomas, won the North's first real victory of the war at Mill Springs, Kentucky. Another branch of the Federal army pushed the Confederates out of Missouri and then won another victory in March at Elkhorn Tavern (or Pea Ridge), Arkansas. In February 1862 Halleck sent 15,000 men under General Ulysses S. Grant, accompanied by a flotilla of gunboats commanded by Andrew Foote, to capture some of the important river forts. Grant, the son of a tanner, had been educated at West Point and had a good record in the Mexican War. However, an unfortunate Western posting had led to him resigning from the army in 1854. After that little had gone right for him. After failing as a real estate agent and as

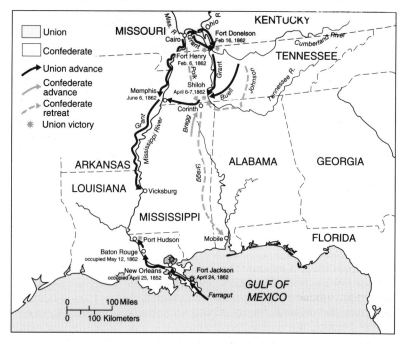

The War in the West

a custom-house clerk, he was back working in his father's store in Galena (Illinois) in 1861. Volunteering for duty, his military experience, plus the support of a local influential politician, ensured that he was quickly promoted to brigadier general. His first engagement at Belmont, while not particularly successful, brought Grant some recognition and convinced him that henceforward he would think more about what he planned to do to the enemy than what the enemy might be planning to do to him.

In February 1862 Grant and Foote captured Fort Henry: Foote's naval bombardment was far more important than Grant's troops. But Union gunships were not sufficient to capture the stronger and more important Fort Donelson. The place was besieged and Grant made it clear he would accept no terms but 'unconditional and immediate surrender'. (Ever afterwards Grant was known as 'U.S.' - 'Unconditional Surrender' - Grant.) Fort Donelson - and its 16,000 garrison - tamely surrendered and Union forces now effectively controlled the Tennessee and Cumberland rivers, vital arteries into the South. Johnston retreated to Corinth, leaving Kentucky and most of Tennessee under Federal control.

In March 1862 General Halleck, aiming to drive further south, sent troops and gunboats to take New Madrid and Island No 10 (both successfully captured), and ordered Grant and Buell to push into south-west Tennessee. In early April 1862 Grant with an army of over 40,000 men, encamped on the west bank of the Tennessee river, near Pittsburg Landing, waiting for Buell's army. But on 6 April 1862 Johnston, who had finally succeeded in concentrating his troops, launched a surprise attack. In the ensuing battle of Shiloh, Confederate forces put many Northerners to flight. Fortunately for Grant enough Federal regiments held out to ensure that the Southerners did not win a total victory. Confederate planning was not helped by the death of Johnston, hit by a bullet in the midst of battle. General Beauregard took over and, as the first day of battle drew to a close, telegraphed to Davis that he had won a 'complete victory'. But Grant, despite his mistakes on the first day, remained calm and with good reason. That night, 25,000 fresh troops from Buell's army arrived. This meant that on the second day the Confederate army was outnumbered 30,000 to 50,000 and after heavy fighting retreated to Corinth.

At Shiloh (a Hebrew word meaning 'place of peace') the Confederates suffered 10,600 and the Union 13,000 casualties. Nearly 5,000 men died - more than the dead in all the USA's previous wars. Blamed for the near disaster on the first day of Shiloh, Grant was reassigned command. He considered resigning from the army but was finally talked out of it by his friend Sherman. Although Shiloh was certainly not Grant's best-fought battle, its outcome was of great importance. The Union had turned back the Confederate bid to regain the initiative in the Mississippi valley. Halleck now assumed full command and advanced - or rather crawled - towards Corinth. (It took him nearly a month to cover 22 miles!) By the time he arrived, Confederate forces had abandoned the town. Davis, displeased by Beauregard's conduct at Shiloh and his evacuation of Corinth, replaced him with General Braxton Bragg. On the Union side, Halleck's appointment as General-in-Chief left Grant in a stronger command position.

Although the Confederacy had lost control of a vast area, Southerners were confident they could recover lost ground. In the late summer of 1862, hopeful that thousands of Kentuckians would flock to the ranks, Bragg advanced into Kentucky. Few Kentuckians joined the Confederates, and failing to make the most of his opportunities, Bragg finally blundered into a Federal army at Perryville in October 1862. The outnumbered Southerners won a tactical victory but Bragg, facing serious supply problems, had to abandon central Kentucky and retreat into Tennessee. Bragg's Kentucky invasion, like Lee's Maryland invasion, raised then dashed Southern hopes.

10 The East: Fredericksburg to Chancellorsville

General Burnside, appointed by Lincoln to command the Army of the Potomac in November 1862, doubted his ability to lead a large army. Events were to prove that his judgement of his own ability was better than Lincoln's. Lincoln hoped that Burnside would make Lee's army his main target: destruction of this army seemed more important than the capture of Richmond. But Burnside, claiming (sensibly) that Lee would have to defend the Confederate capital, targetted Richmond. His plan was simple: his 100,000 men would advance to Fredericksburg and then strike south.

Lee's 75,000 strong army took up a strong position along Marye's Heights behind Fredericksburg. On 13 December Burnside launched a series of suicidal attacks. The battle of Fredericksburg was a total disaster for the North. Union losses amounted to 11,000. Lee's army lost 5,300 - but this figure included men who went home for Christmas after the battle. Burnside, dissuaded from launching more attacks by his senior commanders, pulled back across the Rappahannock. (Lee missed a very good opportunity to attack.) Federal morale, at a very low ebb after Fredericksburg, was not helped when Burnside's attempt to turn Lee's flank in early January 1863 literally got bogged down in mud.

At the end of January 1863 Lincoln replaced Burnside by 'Fighting' Joe Hooker. Hooker was hardly an exemplary character: a man of dubious morals, he had an over-sized ego, a hot temper and was known to be an intriguer. There were even rumours that he intended to set himself up as military dictator. Lincoln was prepared to risk the dictatorship. What he wanted more than anything else was military success. Hooker, unlike Burnside, was not overawed by Lee. 'May God have mercy on General Lee for I will have none,' he declared and set about infusing a new spirit into his army. By April the Army of the Potomac was the largest and best-equipped force ever seen in America. Hooker (with 130,000 men - twice as many as Lee) was ready to try his luck against the Confederate commander. General Sedgewick threatened Lee at Fredericksburg while the bulk of Hooker's army crossed the Rappahannock upstream, threatening Lee's left flank. By 30 April the main Union army had reached Chancellorsville in the heart of the area known as the 'Wilderness'. Unfortunately for Hooker, the Wilderness's scrubby undergrowth made movement and fighting difficult and helped negate Hooker's enormous advantage in numbers.

Lee now showed himself at his most brilliant. Against the advice of most of his staff, he determined to attack. Leaving General Early with 10,000 men to hold Sedgewick, Lee led 50,000 Confederates to meet Hooker. On 2 May, in the face of a greatly superior Union army, Lee did the unthinkable and further divided his army by sending Jackson with 28,000 men to attack Hooker's right flank. Lee, with the remainder of the army, faced Hooker. Hooker, warned of Jackson's march, thought Lee's army was retreating. Then, just before dusk, Jackson attacked. Hooker's right flank fell back in total confusion - but then held. Nightfall brought an end to the fighting - and also an end to Stonewall Jackson. The Confederate hero was mistakenly shot in the left arm by his own men while inspecting the battlefield. Jackson's arm was amputated but he contracted pneumonia and died on 10 May.

Jackson's efforts at least ensured a Confederate victory. Bemused by events, stunned by falling masonry, and possibly either over- or under-stimulated by too much or too little drink (historians cannot agree on this!), Hooker failed to take advantage of the fact that Lee's forces were still divided. Instead he retreated. This enabled Lee to send half his army to head off Sedgewick who had driven Early from Fredericksburg. Sedgewick was duly forced to retreat across the Rappahannock along with the rest of Hooker's army. Lee had achieved what many see as his most impressive victory. Some historians, pointing out that Lee lost a higher proportion of his army (22 per cent to 15 per cent) than Hooker, have questioned whether Chancellorsville was a great victory. This quibbling seems petty. All contemporaries, North and South, regarded Chancellorsville as a spectacular Confederate victory. With far fewer men, Lee had not only held Hooker but forced him to retreat. His army had also inflicted greater casualties on the enemy: Union losses were 17,000 men; Southern losses were 13,000. Although Jackson's death cast a long shadow, Confederate morale was sky high after the battle. Lee believed his troops were invincible. One last push might force a demoralised North to sue for peace.

11 Gettysburg

Lee's victory at Chancellorsville at the very least bought the Confederacy time and gave it some options. Davis's advisers were split on how best to use the Army of Northern Virginia. Some favoured sending forces to help relieve the siege of Vicksburg (see section 12). Others thought a better tactic was to reinforce Bragg's army and launch a major advance through Tennessee and Kentucky which might force the North to end the Vicksburg siege. But Lee would have none of this. Convinced that only victories on Northern soil would force Union leaders to accept Southern independence, Lee argued in favour of an invasion of Pennsylvania. Such a move might help relieve pressure in the West. It would certainly ease pressure in Virginia and would ensure that his men could live at Northern expense. Lee hoped that he might draw the Federal army out into the open and defeat it. That - and/or the capture of a major Northern town - would be a severe blow to Northern morale. After his 12 months of triumph Lee could do no wrong in the eyes of Davis and he got his way.

In June Lee began his advance northwards. Hooker wanted to attack the now largely unprotected Richmond but Lincoln, worried about Washington, insisted that the destruction of Lee's army was a more important objective. The Army of the Potomac, therefore, tried to follow Lee but with little real idea of where he was heading. On 28 June Lincoln replaced Hooker with General George Meade. Meade, an unpretentious, competent soldier from Pennsylvania, was keen to rid his home state of the invaders. Unbriefed by Hooker about the exact state of play, Meade had little time to get to grips with his new command. On 30 June Confederate soldiers, looking for shoes, stumbled across Union forces at the small town of Gettysburg. Both Lee and Meade now ordered all their forces to converge on the town. Thus began the greatest battle yet fought on the American continent.

The first day of the battle - 1 July - belonged to the Confederacy. Union troops were pushed back on to Culp's Hill and Cemetery Hill. Some military historians claim that if Lee had pushed home his attack that evening, he might have triumphed. Others are not so sure: Union troops were well positioned and might easily have resisted a large-scale Confederate attack. Lee had now time to consider his options. It was clear that Meade's army of 85,000 men had positioned itself on a range of hills south and east of Gettysburg - in a fishhook-type alignment. Rather than attack, Longstreet favoured swinging around the Union left flank and finding a strong position in Meade's rear so that the Confederate army was between the Army of the Potomac and Washington. Longstreet believed that Meade would then have no option but to attack - and it was far better to fight a defensive rather than an offensive action. But Lee would have none of this. The two armies were facing each other and Lee declared: 'I am going to whip them here, or they are going to whip me'.

On the second day of Gettysburg serious fighting did not start until well into the afternoon when a reluctant Longstreet attacked the Union left. The Confederates had some success, killing large numbers of Union soldiers who had unwisely advanced into the Peach Orchard. Confederate troops also seized Big Round Top, a hill on the extreme left of the Union position and came very close to capturing the more strategically important Little Round Top. The fighting on Little Round Top was symbolic of Confederate fortunes on 2 July. Confederate forces came close - but not close enough - to victory. They failed to break through in the centre and had no more success on the Northern right. The second day of Gettysburg ended in stalemate.

Lee was still determined to fight and on 3 July decided to launch his main attack on the Union centre. Before the attack, the Confederate artillery blasted the strong Federal positions - to relatively little effect. Then 15,000 men, led by General Pickett, charged up Cemetery Ridge. The charge, one of the most famous episodes in American military history, was a disaster. Most of the Confederates were mown down by Union artillery and rifle fire and only a few score men actually came to blows with Federal forces on top of Cemetery Ridge. In under one hour the Confederates suffered 6,500 casualties. Pickett's charge had failed and his men retreated. Lee had been beaten. In 3 days he had lost 28,000 men - a third of his entire command. (The Union army had lost only 23,000 men.) All hope of invading the North now ended and Lee was forced to retreat back to Virginia (which he did with some skill).

Lee accepted full responsibility for Gettysburg: 'The army did all it could. I fear I required of it impossibilities'. On 8 August 1863 he wrote the following letter to President Davis.

1 I am extremely obliged to you for the attention given to the wants of this army, and the efforts made to supply them. Our absentees are returning, and I hope the earnest and beautiful appeal made to the country, in your proclamation may stir up the virtue of the 5 whole people, and that they may see their duty and perform it. ...

The general remedy for the want of success in a military commander is his removal. This is natural, and in many instances, proper. For, no matter what may be the ability of the officer, if he loses the confidence of his troops disaster must sooner or later 10 ensue.

I have been prompted by these reflections more than once since my return from Pennsylvania to propose to Your Excellency the propriety of selecting another commander for this army. I have seen and heard of expression of discontent in the public journals at 15 the result of the expedition. I do not know how far this feeling extends in the army. My brother officers have been too kind to report it, and so far the troops have been too generous to exhibit it.

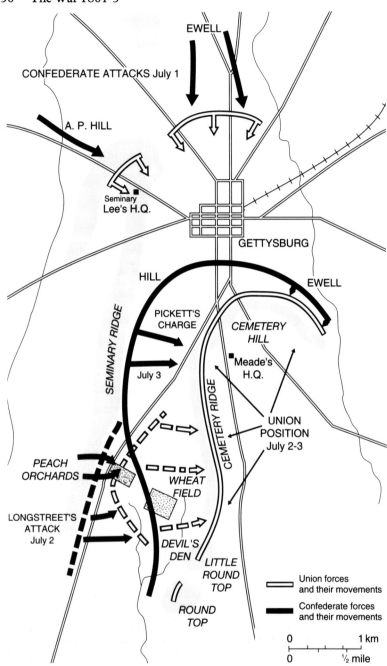

The Battle of Gettysburg, July 1-3 1863

It is fair, however, to suppose that it does exist, and success is so necessary to us that nothing should be risked to secure it. I
20 therefore, in all sincerity request Your Excellency to take measures to supply my place. I do this with the more earnestness because no one is more aware than myself of my inability for the duties of my position. I cannot even accomplish what I myself desire. How can I
25 fulfil the expectations of others? In addition I sensibly feel the growing failure of my bodily strength. I have not yet recovered from the attack I experienced the past spring ... I am so dull that in making use of the eyes of others I am frequently misled. Everything, therefore, points to the advantages to be derived from
30 a new commander, and I the more anxiously urge the matter upon Your Excellency from my belief that a younger and abler man than myself can readily be attained. I know that he will have as gallant and brave an army as ever existed to second his efforts ...

   I have no complaints to make of any one but myself. ... To Your
35 Excellency I am specially indebted for uniform kindness and consideration. You have done everything in your power to aid me in the work committed to my charge, without omitting anything to promote the general welfare.

Davis refused to accept Lee's resignation, replying as follows:

1 Yours of 8th instant has been received. I am glad that you concur so entirely with me as to the want of our country in this trying hour, and am happy to add that after the first depression consequent upon our disaster in the west, indications have appeared that our
5 people will exhibit that fortitude which we agree in believing is alone needful to secure ultimate success ...

   To ask me to substitute you by some one in my judgement more fit to command, or who would possess more of the confidence of the army, or of the reflecting men of the country, is to demand an
10 impossibility. It only remains for me to hope that you will take all possible care of yourself, that your health and strength may be entirely restored, and that the Lord will preserve you for the important duties devolved upon you in the struggle of our suffering country for the independence which we have engaged in war to
15 maintain.

There is no doubt that Gettysburg was a serious defeat for the Confederacy. The myth of Lee's invincibility had been broken and this in itself was a great morale booster for the North. After Gettysburg Lee was never again strong enough to launch a major invasion of the North. But whether Gettysburg was the major turning point of the war is debateable. If Lee had won (and afterwards he maintained he would have won if he had had Jackson) he would have threatened a number of important Northern cities - Harrisburg, Philadelphia, Baltimore and Washington. But it is unlikely that Lee's army, short of ammunition, could have held a single Northern city for any length of time and, given the situation in the West, it seems unlikely that Lincoln's will (or Northern morale in general) would have collapsed.

Defeat at Gettysburg did not make Confederate defeat inevitable. The battle was not strategically decisive, simply because Meade, despite Lincoln's desperate urgings, was unable to follow up his victory. Lee's army regrouped and continued to hold North Virginia. Indeed for the rest of 1863 there were few major engagements on the Virginia front.

Abraham Lincoln ought to have the last word on Gettysburg. In November part of the battlefield was made a permanent cemetery for the soldiers who had fallen there. Lincoln was asked to make 'a few appropriate remarks' and the result was the most memorable of all American addresses.

1 Fourscore and seven years ago our fathers brought forth on this continent a new nation, conceived in Liberty, and dedicated to the proposition that all men are created equal.

  Now we are engaged in a great civil war, testing whether that
5 nation or any nation so conceived and so dedicated can long endure. We are met on a great battlefield of that war. We have come to dedicate a portion of that field as a final resting place for those who here gave their lives that that nation might live. It is altogether fitting and proper that we should do this.
10   But in a larger sense we cannot dedicate - we cannot consecrate - we cannot hallow - this ground. The brave men, living and dead, who struggled here, have consecrated it, far above our poor power to add or detract. The world will little note nor long remember what we say here, but it can never forget what they did here. It is for
15 us the living, rather, to be dedicated here to the unfinished work which they who fought here have thus far so nobly advanced. It is rather for us to be here dedicated to that great task remaining before us - that from these honoured dead we take increased devotion - that we here highly resolve that these dead shall not have
20 died in vain - that this nation, under God, shall have a new birth of freedom - and that government of the people, by the people, for the people, shall not perish from the earth.

12 The West: Vicksburg

Gettysburg was one of two major blows to the South in July 1863. From August 1862 the Confederacy had been trying to hold Vicksburg - the 'Gibraltar of the West'. Confederate control of the town prevented the Union from controlling the Mississippi. In Davis's view Vicksburg was vital to the Confederate cause: it was 'the nailhead that held the South's two halves together'. The town was probably not as important as Davis thought. There was relatively little trade between the two halves of the Confederacy and the Union had to use massive forces to retain control of the Mississippi. Nevertheless Vicksburg did have a symbolic importance. The capture of the town would demoralise the South and sustain the North.

As the Federal threat to Vicksburg grew, Davis appointed Joseph Johnston to oversee Confederate military operations in the West. Unfortunately, Johnston's exact power was illdefined and Bragg (in Tennessee) and Pemberton (at Vicksburg) continued to exercise independent command. Davis's hope was that Johnston would bring a unified vision to the West resulting in the allocation of scarce resources to counter the most dangerous of several Union threats. But Johnston did little to produce such a vision - or even a workable strategy.

General Grant was given the task of taking Vicksburg. His Vicksburg campaign began in earnest in November 1862. Vicksburg's natural defences - not least the Mississippi river - made it difficult to capture. Moreover, Grant faced other major problems: Confederate cavalry constantly threatened his supply line; and command of the Union forces was divided. In late December Grant's attempt to outflank Vicksburg from the north failed when General Sherman was defeated at Chickasaw Bluffs. Over the winter of 1862-3 Grant probed unsuccessfully for a crossing which would enable him to get his forces on the high ground east of the Mississippi. But all his efforts came to nothing.

Finally Grant determined to gamble. Marching his army down the west side of the Mississippi, he relied upon Admiral Porter's ironclad fleet sailing past Vicksburg. This was achieved on the night of 16-17 April 1863 and two weeks later Grant ferried his army, now 30 miles south of Vicksburg, across the Mississippi. The ensuing campaign was brilliant. Aware that he would be outnumbered if the two Confederate forces in the vicinity (Pemberton with 30,000 men at Vicksburg and Johnston with 25,000 men near the Mississippi state capital of Jackson) united, Grant's aim was to defeat the two Confederate armies separately. Largely ignoring his line of communications, he cut inland. In three weeks his army marched 200 miles and won several key battles. One wing of the Union army defeated Johnston and captured the town of Jackson. The other wing defeated Pemberton forcing him to retreat into Vicksburg. After twice failing to storm the Confederate defences, Grant lay siege to Vicksburg. The town was shelled and Confederate troops and civilians became increasingly short of food. Finally on 4 July Vicksburg surrendered. Some 30,000 Confederates were taken prisoner. Five days later Port Hudson, a town further down the Mississippi which had been under siege since mid-May, also surrendered. The Mississippi was now a Union highway and Lincoln could proudly declare that, 'The Father of

Waters again goes unvexed to the sea'.

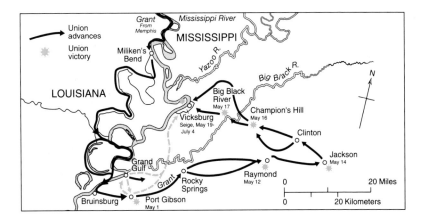

The Vicksburg campaign 1863

13 Tennessee and Chattanooga

The war in 1862-3 was not limited to Virginia and the Mississippi
Valley. There was also important fighting in Tennessee. At the end of
1862 the Union Army of the Cumberland, now commanded by General
Rosecrans tried to drive the Confederate Army of Tennessee, still
commanded by Braxton Bragg, out of Tennessee. On 31 December
Rosecrans and Bragg severely mauled each other at the Battle of
Murfreesboro (or Stones River) near Nashville. Bragg renewed the
battle two days later but his attack was beaten back and he was forced to
withdraw. Both sides suffered terrible casualties. Tennessee then
remained remarkably quiet for six months. The main 'fighting' was the
in-fighting in the Confederate army between the quarrelsome,
quick-to-blame Bragg and most of his Generals. The bitter quarrels
destroyed any *esprit de corps* which remained in the high command of the
Army of Tennessee. Bragg, pedantic and indecisive, had a virtual
nervous breakdown and no Confederate strategy was formulated.

    Lincoln, anxious to press the Confederacy on all fronts, demanded
more decisive action. Rosecrans delayed offensive action until June
1863 when Lincoln threatened him with dismissal. Rosecrans then
moved swiftly, forcing Bragg to retreat 80 miles to Chattanooga, an
important rail centre. Unable to hold the town, Bragg withdrew to
Chickamauga Creek, where he was reinforced by 12,000 men from the
Army of Northern Virginia, led by Longstreet.

    In September Rosecrans advanced south-eastwards in three columns.
Bragg, missing a wonderful opportunity to attack, allowed the Northern
commander to concentrate his forces. On 19-20 September Bragg

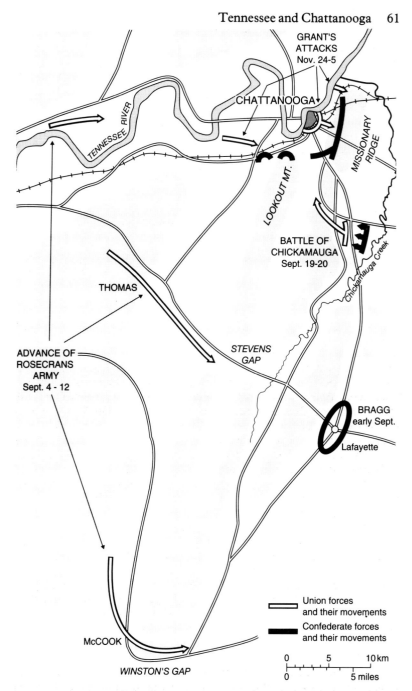

Chickamauga and Chattanooga, September-November, 1863

finally gave battle at Chickamauga Creek. (This was the only major battle in the entire war in which the Confederates actually outnumbered Union forces!) The Confederates came close to winning a major victory. Only a brave rearguard action by General Thomas prevented a rout and enabled the Union army to retreat to Chattanooga. The battle of Chickamauga cost the Confederates nearly 18,500 casualties compared to the Union's 16,500.

Bragg incensed many of his subordinate commanders by failing to follow up the hard-won victory. Instead, he simply besieged Chattanooga. Little was done to cut the frail Union supply line and again there was massive dissension within Bragg's army. Longstreet was appalled at Bragg's conduct: 'I am convinced that nothing but the hand of God can help as long as we have our present commanders,' he said. Davis, aware that the Western high command was almost paralysed, visited the Confederate army outside Chattanooga. After interviewing Bragg and many of his subordinate officers, Davis left Bragg in charge. Bragg's army was weakened by the fact that Longstreet's corps was transferred for a futile move against Knoxville to the north.

Despite Confederate failings, the Federal position in Chattanooga was critical. The Union army was so short of food it seemed it might be forced to surrender. Lincoln, who throughout the war had appreciated the talents of Grant, now gave him command of all Union forces between the Appalachians and the Mississippi. Grant acted swiftly, first establishing the so-called 'cracker line' to Chattanooga. On 24 November Union troops stormed the seemingly impregnable Lookout Mountain. The next day Grant's men overran the Confederate positions on Missionary Ridge. Confederate forces retreated in disarray into Georgia. Weeks too late, Bragg was relieved of his command. He returned to Richmond as Davis's military adviser.

14 Conclusion

The Confederacy had done well to survive the Northern threat in mid-1862. For part of 1862-3 it seemed as though it might actually triumph. But the defeats at Gettysburg, Vicksburg and Chattanooga were severe blows to Southern morale. By December 1863 the situation for the Confederacy in the West seemed desperate. The Union had effectively cut the Confederacy in two and was preparing to invade Georgia. Large areas of Virginia, Tennessee and Louisiana were already under Union control. Nevertheless, the Confederacy was far from beaten. The 'rebel' spirit can perhaps best be summed up by a comment made to Lee by a survivor of Pickett's charge: 'We'll fight them sir, till hell freezes over, and then we'll fight them on the ice'. If the Confederacy could continue to inflict heavy casualties on the Union, there was every chance that the Northern electorate might oust Lincoln in the 1864 presidential election and vote for a peace candidate. There were likely to be opportunities for Confederate forces. Out West the Union faced the problem of long supply lines. In the East the Confederacy still had Lee and the Army of Northern Virginia.

***

Making notes on 'The War 1861-3'

Your notes on this chapter should give you an understanding of the main events of the first two years of the American Civil War. You will need to consult the various maps so that you are familiar with the places mentioned in the text. As you read the chapter try to identify why both the Union and the Confederacy failed to win the war in the first two years. What went wrong? What could either side have done that was different?

***

Source-based questions on 'The War 1861-3'

1 Lee and Davis
Read Lee and Davis's correspondence in August 1863 on pages 55 and 57. Answer the following questions.
a) On what grounds does Lee believe he should be replaced? (3 marks)
b) What did Davis mean by his comment 'our disasters in the west'? (2 marks)
c) What do the letters indicate of Davis's skill as Confederate President? (5 marks)

2 The Gettysburg Address
Read Lincoln's Gettysburg Address on page 58. Answer the following questions.
a) Do you think a wife or mother of a soldier who had died fighting at Gettysburg would have been impressed by Lincoln's speech? Explain your answer. (5 marks)
b) The Gettysburg Address is regarded as the most memorable of all American addresses. Why do you think that is? (5 marks)

CHAPTER 4

The Southern Home Front

1 Introduction

With fewer people, far less in the way of industrial capacity, a less well-developed railway system, and with a Northern blockade disrupting trade with Europe, the odds were stacked heavily against the Confederacy from the start. Moreover, while Lincoln took over a going concern in Washington, Jefferson Davis's administration had to build the Confederate government from scratch. To fight - never mind to win - the war, Southerners would need to make a far greater sacrifice than Northerners. Ultimately the efforts of the Confederate government and the Southern people were in vain. Was this because neither government nor people were equal to the task? Was the Confederate cause lost within the Confederacy itself rather than on the battlefield? Or did the Confederate underdog perform far better on the domestic front than could reasonably have been expected?

2 The Confederate Government

a) Jefferson Davis

Davis, harshly criticised by many Southerners both during and after the war, remains a controversial figure. His Vice-President, Alexander Stephens, thought him, 'weak, timid, petulant, peevish, obstinate' and blamed him for practically everything that went wrong in the Confederacy. Historians continue to berate him. David Potter saw Davis's performance as the most important reason why the Confederacy lost the war, claiming that if Davis and Lincoln had reversed roles, the Confederacy might well have won.

Davis had not wanted to become Confederate President. A Mexican War hero and wealthy Mississippi planter, he had been both a distinguished Senator and an able Secretary of War in the 1850s. Educated at West Point, he felt better qualified for military than political command. Yet even though he disliked the kind of politicking the presidency required, he decided he must do his duty and accept the offer of the office. Some Southerners soon wished he had been less dutiful.

Certainly Davis had his failings. One of these was his inability to establish good working relationships with many of his colleagues, not least Vice-President Stephens who left Richmond in 1862 and rarely spoke to Davis thereafter. As President, Davis seems to have made enemies more easily than friends, quarrelling with both military commanders and leading politicians. He found it hard to work with men who enjoyed less than his full approval and disagreements with him could soon become feuds. Perhaps the high turnover in his cabinet is proof of his inability to cement firm relationships. In the course of the war he appointed no less than four Secretaries of State and six Secretaries of War. This high turnover perhaps also indicates an inability to appoint the right people to the right job. Some of his military appointments, such as General Braxton Bragg and Commissary General Lucius B. Northrop, were disastrous.

Davis is also blamed for constant meddling in the affairs of subordinates, especially in military matters. Finding it hard to prioritise and to delegate, he inevitably got bogged down in trivial detail. Indecision is seen as another of his major failings: lengthy cabinet meetings often came to no conclusion.

Many contemporaries attacked Davis - a pre-war, state-rights Democrat - for having despotic tendencies. Historians, by contrast, have criticised him exercising his executive powers far too sparingly. Some things he ought to have done he could not bring himself to do. For example, although Congress gave him the authority to (virtually) nationalise the Southern railways, he did not do so. Nor did he deal harshly with an increasingly critical Southern press or with opponents within the Confederacy, suspending the writ of habeas corpus only under Congressional authority. He has also been criticised for a failure

POSITION	NAME	DATES OF SERVICE
Attorney General	Judah P. Benjamin	5 Mar - 21 Nov 1861
	Thomas Bragg	21 Nov 1861 - 18 Mar 1862
	Thomas H. Watts	18 Mar 1862 - 1 Oct 1863
	Wade Keyes	1 Oct 1863 - 2 Jan 1864
	George Davis	2 Jan 1864 - 24 Apr 1865
Postmaster General	John H. Reagan	6 Mar 1861 - 10 May 1865
President	Jefferson Davis	18 Feb 1861 - 3 May 1865
Secretary of State	Robert Toombs	21 Feb - 24 July 1861
	Robert M.T. Hunter	24 July 1861 - 22 Feb 1862
	William M. Browne	7 Mar - 18 Mar 1862
	Judah P. Benjamin	18 Mar 1862 - 2 May 1865
Secretary of the Treasury	Christopher Memminger	21 Feb 1861 - 17 July 1864
	George Trenholm	18 July 1864 - 27 Apr 1865
Secretary of War	Leroy Pope Walker	21 Feb - 16 Sept 1861
	Judah P. Benjamin	21 Nov 1861 - 17 Mar 1862
	George Wythe Randolph	18 Mar - 15 Nov 1862
	Gustavus Woodson Smith	17 Nov - 20 1862
	James A. Seddon	21 Nov 1862 - 5 Feb 1865
	John C. Breckinridge	6 Feb - 3 May 1865
Vice President	Alexander H. Stephens	11 Feb 1861 - 11 May 1865

Table 2: The Confederate Cabinet

to communicate effectively, to mobilise public opinion, and thus to build a sense of Confederate nationalism. At a time when the Confederacy needed revolutionary inspiration, he is seen as being too conservative.

However, Davis did and does have his defenders. In general the South called its best to lead its quest for independence and perhaps Davis was one of its best. In 1861 he had a national reputation, and (unlike Lincoln) came to the presidency with useful military and administrative experience. Strong-willed, honourable and honest, he had from the outset a more realistic view of the situation than most Southerners. He never under-estimated the Yankees and expected a long, bloody struggle. Robert E. Lee, the Confederacy's great war hero, praised Davis and said he could think of no one who could have done a better job. The fact that Davis appointed Lee says much for his military good sense. Given his military background, the Confederate President felt competent to intrude into strategical matters and from start to finish showed an excellent overall appreciation of the war. Despite later accusations, he did not over command his forces. To generals he trusted, like Lee, he gave help and considerable freedom.

Despite being a pre-war state rights advocate, Davis almost immediately became a Confederate nationalist, supporting tough measures when necessary, even when these ran contrary to concerns about state rights and individual liberty. Assuming control of all military operations, he set out to create a strong national army. His urgings produced the 1862 Conscription Act which saved the Confederacy as first enlistments expired. He was prepared to impose martial law in areas threatened by Union invasion. He also supported the impressment of supplies needed by Confederate troops and urged high taxes on land, cotton and slaves.

As war eroded the Confederacy, he forced himself to become a much more public figure, making several 'tours' of the Confederacy to try to rekindle flagging faith, and maintaining a prodigious correspondence with critics, friends and governors. He probably did as much as anyone could to create - and hold together - a Southern nation. Although he lacked Lincoln's facility with language, he did speak eloquently of the Confederate cause. Few have questioned his dedication to that cause or the intense work he put into a difficult job, the stress of which increasingly took its toll. (Davis suffered from dyspepsia and a neuralgia which grew worse as the war progressed, leaving him blind in one eye and racked by constant pain.) The Confederacy was always likely to lose. Far from his performance contributing to Confederate defeat, it seems fairer to claim that his leadership ensured that it held out for as long as it did.

b) Davis's Cabinet

The Confederate government was far more than a single man. Davis's cabinet obviously played an important role. In all, Davis made sixteen appointments to head the six Confederate Departments. Judah Benjamin, accounted for three of these as he was appointed, in succession, to Justice, War and State. A brilliant lawyer (the first Jew to hold high political office in the USA), he owed his survival to his immense ability (he was often referred to as 'the brains of the Confederacy') and to his close relationship with Davis; no other adviser had the President's ear so often or so influentially. Benjamin, Stephen Mallory (Secretary of the Navy), and John Reagan (Postmaster General) served in the cabinet from start to finish. But there was substantial turnover in the War and State departments. Most of the turnover arose, not from feuds between Davis and his Secretaries, but as a result of Congressional denunciations of executive performance. Davis invariably resisted calls for the resignation of his Secretaries but Congressional clamour sometimes left him with little option but to accept resignations. Benjamin was usually prepared to take the blame for events, if by so doing he sheltered Davis and assisted the Confederate cause.

Under Davis, the cabinet met frequently and deliberated for hours. Davis usually heeded the advice he was given. For the most part he left his Secretaries to get on with running their Departments, involving himself only in the detailed decision making of the War Department, and even here imposing his views only in military operations.

The Departments set out with the intention of mirroring the activities of those in the pre-war union. But most found their administrative challenges dramatically altered by the Civil War. For example, the Navy Department began the war without a major vessel. The Treasury was hampered by a shortage of gold bullion. Shortages of natural resources and productive capacity led the War Department to break new ground in its attempts at centrally directed economic co-ordination. Easily the largest office, the War Department had over 57,000 civilian employees at its height.

The longest-serving War Secretary was James A. Seddon who served from November 1862 until February 1865. An energetic, clear-thinking man, Seddon, aided by his capable Assistant Secretary John Campbell, overseered the myriad details of running the war. Some of Seddon's subordinates were incompetent, not least Commissary General Northrop, responsible for furnishing - or in his case often not furnishing - the armies with supplies. But generally the nine bureaus which made up the War Department were staffed by some of the ablest men in the South. Josiah Gorgas, head of the Ordnance Bureau, performed logistical miracles. He and his well-chosen subordinates did more than any other supply agency to sustain the Confederacy, ensuring that after 1862 Confederate forces were rarely without arms or gunpowder.

Davis's cabinet is often seen as less efficient than that of Lincoln. But most of Davis's appointments were capable men and the various Departments generally attracted effective civil servants. Despite a lack of resources, government operations functioned reasonably smoothly for much of the war.

c) The Confederate Congress

The Confederate Congress played an important role in government. Congressmen in the first, single-house, Provisional Congress (which met in 1861-2) were selected by their state conventions or legislatures rather than being chosen directly by the people. After this, there were two popularly elected Congresses, the first from 1862-4, the second from 1864-5, each consisting of a House and Senate. Of the 267 men who served as Confederate senators or representatives, about a third had been members of the US Congress at one time or another and one - Tyler - had been a US President. The men, and families, who had taken the lead in politics before the war for the most part continued to do so.

Unlike the North, there was no two-party system in the Confederacy. Instead men who had once been bitter political enemies tried to present a united front to the enemy. Many Southerners saw the lack of an 'official' opposition as a good thing which would help maintain Southern unity. But most historians believe that the absence of a two-party system meant that there was less channelling of political activity, less consensus and more squabbling. Davis, moreover, had no party organisation to separate friends from foes, to mobilise support or to help him formulate legislative policy and guide bills through Congress.

Congress often found itself on the horns of a dilemma. While wanting to pass measures which would ensure victory for the Confederacy, it was aware of its 'sacred heritage' to preserve state rights. These two principles frequently clashed. During the first year of the war, most Congressmen rallied round their leader: not to do so smacked of treason. In consequence, the administration's measures - even those seen as draconian and anti-state rights - went through Congress almost intact. However, as morale on the home front deteriorated under the impact of military setbacks, inflation, conscription, impressment and terrible casualty lists, opposition grew, both inside and outside Congress. This was reflected in the 1863 Congressional elections. Southern voters turned away from the original secessionists, voting instead for men who had opposed secession in 1861. Almost 40 per cent of the 137 members of the Second Congress were new to that body. By no means all the new men were opposed to Davis. But many were. Of the 26 senators in the new Congress, 12 were identified with the opposition.

The anti-Davis faction defies easy categorisation. Some opponents held extreme state-rights views, others disagreed with the way the war was being waged. A small minority wanted peace and a restoration of the Union. But there is little evidence of bloc voting and most congressmen voted as their conscience dictated. As the war progressed Davis grew increasingly dependent on the support of congressmen from areas under Union control. Regular elections were impossible in these areas and so most incumbents continued in office. They could vote in full confidence that their constituents would not feel the effects of harsh impressment, sweeping conscription or suspension of civil liberties.

d) States and State Rights

To wage a successful war, the Confederacy had to have the full co-operation of all its states. It also needed a central government strong enough to make the most of all the South's available human and material resources. But some state leaders were not keen to concede too much power to the Confederate government. Appealing to the principle of state rights (for which they had seceded), they resisted many of the efforts of Davis's administration to centralise the running of the war effort.

Over the years a number of historians have echoed the historian Frank Owsley's claim that the Confederacy 'Died of State Rights' and shown that some states did not work for the common cause. Governors Joseph Brown of Georgia and Zebulon Vance of North Carolina are usually seen as leading the often strident protests against centralisation and hindering the war effort by their obstructional activities. Brown, for example, opposed conscription and exempted thousands of Georgians from the draft by enrolling them in bogus state militia units. Vance, more concerned with the defence of North Carolina than with the defence of the Confederacy as a whole, retained uniforms, shoes and blankets for North Carolina's state troops at a time when they were desperately needed by Lee's forces.

In reality, however, the issue of state rights played only a small part in bringing about the Confederacy's defeat. Most state governments were remarkably loyal to the Confederacy and co-operated effectively with the Richmond government. Most of the 28 men who served as Confederate governors were former Democrats and all but three had advocated secession. All were committed to the Confederate cause - including Brown and Vance. Brown, an ardent secessionist and able administrator, rallied Georgians to the war effort. Vance opposed Davis but supported the war, despite fierce opposition to it in some parts of North Carolina.

State governors tended to be more 'nationalist' than their legislatures. As Commanders-in-Chief of their states, they had more power in war than in peace and were not averse to using this power. They initiated most of the necessary legislation at state level - impressing slaves, restricting cotton planting and even declaring martial law. As a result, they often found themselves vying more with their own state legislatures than with Richmond. But usually they got their legislatures to comply with their actions. Thus the national pattern of executive dominance became the state pattern.

Throughout the war, Southern newspapers complained that the state legislatures were filled with incompetents. This resulted to some extent from the press's dissatisfaction with the legislators' inability to remedy the problems caused by the war. But such comments also reflected a real vacuum of experience and talent in state and local politics. Ambitious men who would ordinarily have entered politics chose instead to try to make their names in the military.

e) 'Died of Democracy'?

In February 1862 Davis proclaimed that his administration would continue to cherish and preserve the personal liberties of citizens and boasted that, in contrast to the North, 'there has been no act on our part to impair personal liberty or the freedom of speech, of thought or of the press'. Protecting individual rights might seem an important aim (albeit an unusual one for a state who's cornerstone was slavery!). However, the historian David Donald has claimed that concern for individual liberties cost the Confederacy the war. Unwilling to take tough action against internal dissent, the Confederacy, in Donald's view, 'Died of Democracy'.

Donald's argument, however, is not convincing. The notion that the Confederacy could somehow have created a great government machine which could have suppressed civil liberties - and that if it had done so it might have won the war - is nonsense. Davis, like the vast majority of Southerners, was fighting for what he saw as traditional American values: he could not easily abandon those values. To have done so would have alienated the public whose support was essential for military success.

Donald's supposition that the Confederacy allowed total individual freedom is also mistaken. In February 1862 Congress authorised Davis to suspend the writ of habeas corpus and to declare martial law in areas threatened by the enemy. Davis immediately placed Confederate front-line towns under military rule. The widespread opposition to conscription convinced Congress to permit Davis to suspend the right of habeas corpus on three separate occasions for a total of 16 months. These suspensions and the use of martial law were justified as necessary for apprehending thousands of draft evaders.

Elements of the fiercely independent Southern press were critical, not just of the (perceived) violation of civil rights, but of virtually all Davis's policies. Davis, while expressing the view that 'the public journals' were 'generally partisan' and 'venal', did not interfere with the press and seems never to have used his powers to arrest opposition newspaper editors, proprietors or reporters. Several editors, defending the principle of free speech, ignored 1862 censorship restrictions and even published news about Confederate military activity. Neither national nor state authorities succeeded in suppressing outspoken journals.

But to imply that there was total freedom of speech would be false. The War Department, which had initially relied upon the discretion of journalists and editors, gradually tightened its restrictions on military reporting, controlling information sent over the telegraph and through the mail. Confederate commanders effectively closed their camps to journalists. In lieu of specific legislation, public pressures that had long stifled discussion about slavery generally succeeded in imposing loyalty to the Confederacy. Opposition newspapers could find their presses destroyed by vigilantes. Preachers and teachers who questioned the course of events were liable to lose their jobs - and even their lives. In the first years of war Unionists in the South had little option but to keep their views to themselves or to flee northwards.

In conclusion, it seems unlikely that the preservation of basic freedoms - in so far as they were preserved - had more than a marginal impact on the demise of the Confederacy. In fact, it could be argued that the preservation of civil liberties and democratic processes in war is as much a strength as a weakness. Certainly, President Lincoln's concern about such matters did not prevent Northern victory.

f) Voluntary Association

Much of what was achieved in the Confederacy was due more to local and private initiative than to government order. Men who led the local community were likely to lead either on the battlefield or on the home front. Planters often organised and outfitted local regiments with their own money. During the initial mobilisation in 1861 most Southern states relied on local communities to supply the troops with basic necessities. Churches played a particularly important role. Most Southern clergymen, whether Protestant or Catholic, supported the war: many clergy preached and wrote in defence of the new nation. Church buildings often became centres for Confederate rallies and for women's groups who made clothing, flags and other materials for the troops. Women also helped found Church-related hospitals and organised Home Missionary Societies to care for slaves, feed the poor, and help orphans.

As men marched off to war, women played an increasingly important role in terms of managing the home front. Without female support the Confederacy would soon have collapsed. By mid-1862 it is true that fewer and fewer women were willingly sending their men off to war: many attempted to prevent them being drafted, tried to get them discharged, or even encouraged desertion. But until the winter of

1864-5 most women seemed to have remained committed to the value systems of the old South and to upholding Southern nationalism for which they, like their menfolk, were willing to accept colossal sacrifice.

3 Financing the War

Christopher Memminger, Treasury Secretary from 1861 to 1864, faced the problem of paying for the war effort. A South Carolinian lawyer with only limited experience in financial affairs before 1861, Memminger was honest, hard working and committed to the Confederate cause. However, historians such as Douglas Ball are convinced that the Confederacy's greatest failure was in the area of finance, and have held Memminger as chiefly responsible.

In fairness to Memminger, the Confederacy was always likely to find it difficult to finance a long war. In 1861 it had few gold reserves and much of the South's capital was tied up in land and slaves. The Northern blockade made it difficult for the South to sell cotton (its greatest asset) and to raise money by raising tariffs. Raising taxes by other means was also fraught with difficulty. The only machinery for collecting taxes lay with the individual states and Southerners had no tradition of paying direct taxes.

In 1861 most Confederate officials, believing that the war would be short, hoped it could be financed through import and export duties. Tariffs were levied on a variety of goods and a tax placed on all ships entering Southern ports. These duties, however, failed to bring in enough money. Memminger, therefore, soon advocated the imposition of a direct tax on real property. But Congress - fearing popular disapproval - balked. Not until April 1863 did Congress levy taxes on occupation, income, profits, produce and property. But this - and other - direct tax laws still failed to bring in sufficient revenue. State governments, which raised the taxes, were often reluctant to send money to Richmond. Rather than tax their citizens, states often borrowed money or printed it in the form of state notes to pay their dues, thus worsening inflationary pressures.

In an effort to feed the Southern troops, Congress passed the Impressment Act in March 1863 and the Tax-in-kind Act in April 1863. The Impressment Act, which allowed the seizure of goods to support the armies at the front line, legalised what the armies and various supply bureaus were already practising. Even when the Confederate government 'paid' for impressed supplies, it did so at rock-bottom prices and with promissory notes which were essentially worthless. In many areas, army officials still did not bother with the formality of payment of any kind.

The Taxation-in-kind Act, which authorised government agents to collect 10 per cent of agricultural produce from all Southern farmers, was perhaps the most unpopular act the Confederacy ever passed. The collecting agents, who often preyed on the most defenceless, were loathed and farmers did all they could to resist paying arbitrarily set quotas. Davis accepted the unfairness of the Act but thought it justified by 'absolute necessity'. He may have been right. Taxation-in-kind did help supply Confederate armies during the last two years of the war - despite the fact that much of the collected food rotted at depots before it could be transported to the armies.

As well as raising Confederate taxes, individual states also levied their own taxes. States experimented with a variety of taxes - on slaves, luxury items, corporation profits, income tax - but they were usually inefficiently collected. Although there was an apparent increase in total tax revenues, such proceeds when converted into gold dollars showed an actual decline in real revenue. This was because state tax rates failed to keep pace with inflation. Most states, like the Confederate Congress, were unwilling to put public sentiment to the test of severe tax increases. Taxation rates, therefore, were generally too light. Only 8 per cent of the Confederacy's income was derived from taxes as compared with 20 per cent of the Union's.

The less the Confederate authorities taxed, the more they had to borrow. As early as February 1861 the Confederate Provisional Congress, confident that loans would be an effective way of paying for the war, allowed Memminger to raise $15 million in bonds and stock certificates. Guaranteed with cotton, there were initially many loan and bond subscribers, both within the Confederacy and abroad. The most famous foreign loan was the $15 million Erlanger loan, finally agreed in January 1863. This loan restored Southern credit abroad and allowed Southern agents to contract for more war material. But after 1863, when the tide of battle turned against the Confederacy, most European financiers were reluctant to risk loaning money to what seemed increasingly like a lost cause. After the initial enthusiasm of 1861, attempts at selling bonds within the Confederacy had only limited success.

Given that the Confederacy was able to raise only about one third of its war costs through taxes, bonds and loans, Memminger had little option but to print vast amounts of Treasury notes to cover most of the Confederacy's expenditure. Most Southerners supported the issue of Confederate paper notes. By mid-1861 all Southerners were used to paper currency and a currency put out by the central government, rather than by states or banks, seemed to be the best available. Unfortunately for Memminger's reputation, the Confederate government steadily enlarged the amount of Treasury notes authorised. It also failed to centralise the printing of money and bring it under government control. Individual states, towns, counties, banks and railway companies continued to issue paper notes. The result was that the Confederacy was soon awash with paper. (The situation was not helped by considerable counterfeiting, some of which was encouraged by the North.) By early

1864 the Treasury did not know how many notes were in circulation. Inflation was soon out of control. (Shortages of basic commodities, resulting from the malfunctioning of the railway system and by the Union blockade, also helped push up prices.) By December 1863 the general price index in the eastern Confederacy was over 2,000 times what it had been in January 1861: by 1865 that index was over 5,000 times the 1861 level. Inflation undoubtedly resulted in widespread suffering, particularly for those working for the government, whose wages did not keep pace with rising prices. All the Confederate government's efforts to retard or reverse inflation proved inadequate. Attempts to fix prices, for example, merely added to the inflationary spiral by encouraging hoarding and thus exacerbating shortages of vital produce.

The failure to develop an adequate tax law, massive inflation, a spiraling debt and other financial problems forced Memminger to resign - in disgrace - in 1864. His successor, George Trenholm, tried to reduce the amount of money in circulation but by 1864-5 the Confederacy was on its last legs and the financial situation was desperate. By 1865 the Confederate government was over $800 million in debt and state governments had also accumulated massive debts.

Many scholars have agreed with Douglas Ball that misguided Confederate fiscal policies (especially during the first months of the war) were a major cause of Confederate defeat. Hyper-inflation is seen as eroding the Southern will to continue the struggle. But perhaps the financial mistakes have been over stressed. It is unlikely that a fully comprehensive fiscal programme could have been effected in 1861-2. High taxes would have been bitterly resented and possibly counter productive. When Congress did levy direct taxes on all real and personal

"The Results of Extortion and Speculation.—The state of affairs brought about by the speculating and extortion practiced upon the public cannot be better illustrated than by the following grocery bill for one week for a small family, in which the prices before the war and those of the present are compared:

1860		1863	
Bacon, 10 lbs. at 12½¢........	$1.25	Bacon, 10 lbs. at $1.........	$10.00
Flour, 30 lbs. at 5¢...........	1.50	Flour, 30 lbs. at 12½¢.......	3.75
Sugar, 5 lbs. at 8¢...........	.40	Sugar, 5 lbs. at $1.15........	5.75
Coffee, 4 lbs. at 12½¢........	.50	Coffee, 4 lbs. at $5..........	20.00
Tea (green), ½ lb. at $1......	.50	Tea (green), ½ lb. at $16....	8.00
Lard, 4 lbs. at 12½¢.........	.50	Lard, 4 lbs. at $1...........	4.00
Butter, 3 lbs. at 25¢.........	.75	Butter, 3 lbs. at $1.75.......	5.25
Meal, 1 pk. at 25¢..........	.25	Meal, 1 pk. at $1...........	1.00
Candles, 2 lbs. at 15¢........	.30	Candles, 2 lbs. at $1.25......	2.50
Soap, 5 lbs. at 10¢..........	.50	Soap, 5 lbs. at $1.10........	5.50
Pepper and salt (about)......	.10	Pepper and salt (about).....	2.50
Total................. $6.55		Total............... $68.25	

"So much we owe the speculators, who have stayed at home to prey upon the necessities of their fellow-citizens."

Inflation in Richmond 1860-63

property (in 1864), they proved difficult to collect and simply caused massive protests. It remains an astonishing fact that the Confederacy was able to finance a war for four years.

4 The Confederate Economy

The Confederacy faced major economic problems in 1861. Overwhelmingly rural and heavily dependent on cotton, the South had only one city (New Orleans) of over 50,000 people and relatively little industry. In 1860 Southern manufacturing capacity was only about one-twelfth that of the North. The Confederacy's transportation system was also less well developed: it had only a third of the nation's rail mileage, employed less than a fifth of the country's railway workers and was short of locomotives, rolling stock and track materials. Communication was not helped by the fact that there were more than a hundred railway companies, using a variety of different gauges.

Despite the Confederacy's industrial weakness, Confederate leaders were confident that foreign purchases and development of the South's own resources could provide all that was needed to equip Southern forces. In 1861 purchasing agents, working for both the Confederate government and individual states, were sent to Europe to buy essential military equipment. In many respects the Confederate government also acted forcefully to place the South's economy on a war footing and to expand its existing industrial infrastructure. Before the war most Southerners took the view that economic development was beyond the proper scope of the central government's powers. But after 1861 Confederate government officials, working largely through the War Department's assorted bureaus, intruded into almost every aspect of economic life as regulations abounded to manage conscription, impressment, taxation, manufacturing and transportation. The result was a 'quasi-nationalised' economy, with the Richmond government directing the production and distribution of much of the South's war materials and playing a much greater role in economic matters than Lincoln's government did in the North. 'Confederate socialism' came about, not because Davis and his cabinet embraced socialist economic theories but simply because centralisation policies seemed the best way to mobilise and fight the war. The Ordnance Bureau, brilliantly led by Josiah Gorgas, a Northerner who stayed loyal to his Southern wife rather than to his native state of Pennsylvania, played a crucial role, creating what has been termed a 'military-industrial complex'. Ensuring that there were armament works in virtually every Confederate state, he exerted increasing control over private enterprises. By 1863 there were enough arsenals, factories and gunpowder works in the South to keep the Confederate armies supplied with the basic tools of war. The Ordnance Bureau continued providing munitions to Confederate forces until April 1865. No other Southern supply bureau achieved so much.

During the war the Confederate government intervened in communications and transport matters. In 1861 Congress gave Davis the authority to control the Southern telegraph network. The War Department also assumed increasing control over the South's railway system. Companies were required to share equipment, spare parts and rolling stock. Railway schedules were regulated. Draft exemptions were issued to ensure that railway companies had skilled workers. The government even built three short but important connecting lines.

The Confederacy also took forceful steps to regulate foreign commerce. At the start of the war, Confederate authorities let private companies and state governments monopolise the lucrative business of blockade running. But by the autumn of 1861 the government started to acquire a small blockade-running fleet of its own. In 1863 Congress passed a law requiring all blockade runners to carry at least one-third of their cargo on government account. This meant the ships had to carry government cotton out and bring war supplies in - or face confiscation. This was followed up in February 1864 by a ban on the importation of luxury goods without a special permit. Davis was also given the authority to regulate all cotton shipments. By cutting out the middlemen, the Confederate government was able to sell cotton abroad and buy military supplies with the proceeds.

Blockade running was remarkably successful. Hundreds of ships - some state owned, some Confederate government owned, but most owned by private individuals from the Confederacy and Britain - were engaged at one time or another. The most popular routes were from Nassau in the Bahamas to Charleston and from Bermuda to Wilmington. The blockade runners, most of which were specially built in Britain, had the advantage of surprise and speed. It is estimated that they stood a 75 per cent chance of success. This high success rate continued until the last months of the war, despite an increasingly tighter Union blockade. Overall, the South imported 60 per cent of its small arms, 30 per cent of its lead, 75 per cent of its saltpetre and nearly all its paper for making cartridges.

State governments also played an important economic role. Most manufactured and distributed salt, a product that was in short supply. Some tried to regulate the distribution of other scarce goods. Others made contracts with manufacturers to try to prevent speculators from cornering supplies. Most tried to ensure that Southern farmers shifted from cotton cultivation to food production. State agents, with the help of local vigilante committees, enforced the laws. The result was a reduction in the cotton crop - from over 4,000,000 bales in 1861 to only 300,000 bales in 1864.

However, 'Confederate socialism' should not be exaggerated. In the final analysis, most of what was achieved on the economic front was the result of private initiative rather than of Confederate or state government order. Davis's government mainly confined its activities to the military sphere and did little for the civilian sector of the economy. Even on the military side, private enterprise was crucial. The Tredegar Ironworks at Richmond, the South's largest industrial complex and its leading ordnance producer, remained in private control.

However, not all historians are convinced that the Confederacy did as well as it might have done economically. Some claim that the Confederate government's attempts to interfere in all aspects of economic life was a major weakness. Short of trained personnel, the Richmond bureaucracy was simply not up to the task of carrying out many of its ambitious schemes and ultimately was unable to meet either the military or civilian needs of the Confederacy. Some scholars claim that the Confederacy actually overmobilised its military effort, stripping away so much from civilian production that the home front collapsed.

More perhaps could and should have been done to oversee the railways. The Confederate government, aware of state rights concerns, failed to provide strong supervision of the railway system as a whole. Handicapped by a shortage of materials and labour, the South was unable to maintain its railway network. The result was that raw materials destined for factories and foodstuffs bound for armies or towns were often left at depots for want of transport.

The Confederacy might also have used 'King Cotton' to better effect, especially in the first months of the war. The 'informal' embargo on cotton exports - supported - but never officially sanctioned - by the Confederate government - may have been a mistake. Its aim was two-fold: to ensure that planters turned to food production: and to create an artificial cotton scarcity for the purposes of bargaining for foreign recognition (see Chapter 7). Although more food was produced, the embargo failed to have much impact on Britain or France: it simply resulted in the South having vast stockpiles of virtually worthless cotton. Had this been exported early in 1861 (when the Northern blockade was virtually non-existent), the money from the proceeds could have been used to purchase essential war equipment. Instead Southern agents in Europe in 1861 were handicapped by lack of funds and often outbid by Northern competitors who were also seeking to buy up European weapons.

After 1861, government attempts to limit the amount of cotton grown were not totally successful. Although many planters did turn to producing wheat, corn and beans, a minority, appreciating the vast profits to be made, refused to toe the patriotic line. Some, ignoring government orders, smuggled their cotton to Europe through Texas and Mexico. Others, ignoring an 1861 ban, traded with Union merchants who, given the cotton shortage, were prepared to pay staggeringly high prices.

The Confederate government could certainly have taken action sooner to put its foreign requisition house in order and done more to control shipments on the blockade-running ships. Before 1863, many blockade runners were more concerned with making money than with helping the Confederacy, often bringing in luxury goods rather than munitions and other necessities. By the time Davis's government got its blockade-running act together, most Southern ports had been captured or were effectively closed.

The Confederacy might also have used slaves to better effect. Given that many plantations turned to food production which was less labour intensive than cotton growing, more slaves could have been impressed into government service and used for non-combat labour. But most planters had no wish to have their valuable property put at risk. They saw impressment as an issue of principle. The South was fighting for the right of slave owners to control their property. To impress slaves against their owners' wishes was an attack on this principle. Although many slaves were impressed by state governments, the political power of the planter aristocracy ensured that Congress did not authorise Confederate impressment of slaves until 1863-4.

By 1864 all Confederate bureaus were faced with problems that would not go away. Machinery and spare parts were wearing out and could not be replaced, first because raw materials were lacking, and second because the Union blockade was more effective. Indigenous sources of raw materials were steadily lost as Union forces took over large areas of the South. The breakdown of the railway system, much of which was destroyed by Union armies rampaging through the South, proved decisive in the final demise of the Confederacy. By 1865 the South could no longer supply its armies and was facing economic ruin.

5 The Social Impact of the War

Most Southerners had gone to war to preserve a way of life that precluded change. Ironically the war was to lead to massive changes in that way of life. Some of the changes came about because of the total nature of the war: others occurred as a result of defeat. Few of the changes, as far as white Southerners were concerned, were pleasant.

The Confederacy succeeded in mobilising about 900,000 men - over 40 per cent of its white males of fighting age. This had important implications for all aspects of Southern life. It particularly affected the role of women. Most wives of yeoman farmers, as well as facing the constant threat of widowhood, had the immediate task of providing enough food for themselves and their families. This meant working even longer hours and practising strict domestic economy to conserve scarce resources. Wives of planters faced a different challenge. Although less likely to face the threat of hunger, they had to somehow manage large plantations and control increasingly restless slaves. In towns women took over many jobs which had been traditionally done by men. They were invariably paid much less than men and hyper-inflation reduced their purchasing power further. But most working women seem to have accepted their lot.

The war also affected the institution of slavery (see Chapter 6). Although there was no great slave revolt, large numbers of slaves fled their plantations whenever it was safe to do so. Historian James Roark has suggested that, 'Slavery did not explode; it disintegrated ... eroded plantation by plantation, often slave by slave, like slabs of earth slipping into a Southern stream'. By the winter of 1864-5 slave-owners often had to negotiate with the blacks who remained in order to get them to work.

Shortages of basic commodities, inflation, impressment and tax-in-kind had a demoralising effect on all parts of the South. Some areas were also devastated by Union troops. As a Northern policy of 'total war' emerged after mid-1862, Southern citizens suffered increasingly greater deprivation over an ever-broadening area. Sherman's marches through Georgia and the Carolinas in 1864-5 left a huge swathe of destruction: so too (and at the same time) did Sheridan's army in the Shenandoah Valley. But it was not just Union troops who inflicted damage. Confederate troops could also devastate an area. By the winter of 1864-5 the social order had collapsed in some parts of the South as Union raiders, guerilla bands, Confederate deserters and fugitive slaves roamed the countryside, searching for food, looting and wantonly destroying. To have crops taken or property destroyed by 'friends' rather than foes created conflicting loyalties.

Black and white refugees flooded the South as slaves fled their owners and whites fled contesting armies. Black refugees usually headed towards the nearest Union army. White refugees usually made their way to homes of relatives or drifted into the nearest town. The refugee situation became particularly acute in Virginia.

In an effort to tackle the problem of refugees - and poverty in general - both Confederate and state governments, local and town authorities, plus private charities and wealthy individuals became involved in unprecedented relief efforts. Little had been spent on poor relief before the war and a stigma had been attached to those who received it. But events created such distress among civilians that individual welfare was increasingly considered to be a government responsibility. All states tried to allocate money or food to soldiers' families. Yet by the winter of 1864-5 the scale of the problem was so great that it overwhelmed the relief activities. In some states a quarter of the white citizens were dependent on relief by 1865. Previously proud and self-reliant people were now plunged into poverty and unable to provide for themselves. This experience, as well as being physically harsh, was also psychologically painful for thousands of Southerners. The inadequacy of poor relief and the fact it was necessary did great damage to the Confederate cause. Refugees, disheartened by their treatment in towns like Richmond, often drifted back to their homes, even if this meant they had to live under military occupation.

6 Opposition to the War

Many non-slaveholders in the upland areas of the South opposed secession from the start. There was so much support for the Union in East Tennessee and West Virginia that both areas effectively seceded from the Confederacy. This was a substantial drain on Southern manpower: worse still was the fact that some 60,000 white men from these areas, and a further 30,000 or so from other Southern states, actually joined the Union army. Nevertheless, most white Southerners rallied to the Confederate cause in 1861: pro-Union sympathies were a small minority.

But as the war continued, opposition increased. The introduction of conscription in April 1862 was a major cause. Henceforward all white males between the ages of 18 and 35 (soon raised to 45 and then 50) were liable for military service. There were some exceptions. People working in crucial occupations were exempted. So too were white men who could demonstrate that they were in a managerial role on a plantation with 20 slaves or more. Draftees, if they had sufficient wealth, could also hire substitutes from the pool of men not liable for military service. The (three) Conscription Acts, while ensuring that the Confederacy maintained its military strength, resulted in deep division within the South. There were heated debates over state rights. But the implementation of the draft also led to other problems. Lukewarm Confederates now faced a choice of military service or overt opposition. As the war ground on, organised resistance to conscription intensified, especially in the mountain regions of North Carolina and Alabama. Armed men joined together to help one another in eluding the enrollment officers and to fight them off when necessary. This process concentrated disaffection in the very areas that had always opposed secession. Given that the most enthusiastic Confederate supporters had departed to join the army, bands of draft evaders - and deserters - dominated some areas of the South.

Moreover, the Conscription Acts may have fuelled class conflict. Many ordinary white farmers resented the fact that rich Southerners could avoid military service by either hiring substitutes or exempting themselves by the 'Twenty Slave Law'. In reality relatively few wealthy Southerners actually exempted themselves: indeed they were more likely to fight and die than poor Southerners. But the perception of blatant class favouritism rankled. The 'Twenty Slave Law' evoked such criticism that it was soon revised. From May 1863 the overseers' clause pertained only to plantations belonging to minors, women or disabled planters. In addition the law required the plantation's owner to pay $500 to the Confederate Treasury.

Some historians have claimed that the war exacerbated class divisions. Escott's study of North Carolina, for example, suggested that class conflicts (which had existed before 1861) resulted in serious opposition to the (perceived) planter-led Confederacy. Certainly, significant numbers of non-slaveholding men and women became increasingly restive under Confederate rule. However, not all historians are convinced that the opposition was essentially 'class'-based. Non-slaveholding families tended to be concentrated in areas not suitable to plantation agriculture, especially the Appalachian and Ozark mountains. These upland areas of the Confederacy were those that became most disaffected - but they had been disaffected from the start. It is difficult, in consequence, to separate regional differences from class divisions.

Although most overt resistance to the Confederacy occurred in the mountains, as the war dragged on support eroded elsewhere too. Yeoman farmers, who made up the bulk of the Southern population, increasingly felt they bore a disproportionate share of the war's privations. Military service removed a major portion of their labour force. Inflation and shortages added to the woes of their families. Complaints of a 'rich man's war and a poor man's fight' mounted.

In the cities, swollen with refugees, rampant inflation and food shortages prompted repeated unrest. In 1864 there were a number of serious strikes which usually ended with the Confederate government threatening to draft striking workers. Food riots occurred in Mobile, Atlanta and in Richmond in 1863. Poor Southerners resented the fact that some rich hoarders and speculators actually prospered from inflation and shortages.

It was not just poor and yeomen families who were disaffected. As government measures reached more and more deeply into civilian life, planter support for the Confederacy also diminished. Planters disliked being told what they could grow and who they could trade with: they also disliked the impressment of their slaves. As the war progressed many withdrew sullenly to their plantations and did what they could to help themselves, including evading conscription and planting cotton rather than corn.

As hopes of victory became increasingly remote, a peace movement arose within the Confederacy. This movement was a haven for a wide variety of groups. Some wanted independence and criticised Davis for not making more efforts to negotiate with Lincoln. (The criticism was unfair. Davis knew that Lincoln would not except secession under any circumstances.) Others favoured peace even if Southern independence had to be sacrificed.

There was no unified opposition party within Congress. To a greater extent than perhaps at any previous time in American history, Congressmen seem to have genuinely voted according to their consciences on most issues. As a result no single consistently identifiable opposition grouping ever emerged. Instead, there were a number of opposition factions within Congress. The individual most commonly identified as the leader of the opposition was Senator Wigfall of Texas.

But many of Davis's opponents, both in and out of Congress, took their cues from a triumvirate of Georgians - Vice-President Stephens, Governor Brown and Robert Toombs. These men did everything in their power to embarrass the President and discredit his policies.

Nevertheless, it is possible to exaggerate the scale and extent of the opposition. Opposition groups were always a minority in the Confederate Congress. It is also possible to exaggerate the significance of class differences within the Confederacy. Most - non-slaveholding - Southerners remained committed to the Confederate cause - and slavery - until the end. They supported slavery for the same reasons they had always supported it: it was part of the Southern way of life; and it kept the blacks in their place. Hatred of slaveholders and class resentment were not the main reasons why the loyalty of 'plain folks' to the Confederacy wavered. Southerners' will to fight faded only after they had been battered into submission by a stronger military force.

7 Conclusion

The Civil War was far more 'total' in the South than it was in the North. It was thus a 'people's war'. Morale was as crucial on the home front as on the battlefield. Southern morale seems to have been generally high in the first two years of the war, helped by a good harvest in 1861, battlefield success and the hope of European assistance. However, military reverses - and huge casualties - helped undermine the initial confidence. Increasing and often severe hardship on the domestic front further damaged morale. There was an understandable, if not necessarily justified, loss of faith in the Confederate leadership. More and more Southerners decided the price of independence was too high. By 1864-5 many thought their homestead was more important than their homeland.

Davis's government has inevitably been blamed for the way it ran the war. Certainly it made mistakes. But arguably it was no more mistake prone than Lincoln's government. Nor were Southerners less dedicated than Yankees. Most Southerners fought hard and long for their new nation, enduring far greater suffering and hardship than Northerners. The reality was that the South simply had less room for error. Given its 'small battalions', the Confederacy needed to have better leadership, greater financial and economic initiative and more unity than its stronger adversary. Although ultimately not equal to the mighty challenge, the Confederacy's efforts on the home front were, in most respects, better than might have been expected. The bitter truth was that most of its domestic problems were essentially insurmountable.

Making notes on 'The Southern Home Front'

This chapter is designed to show what domestic problems the Confederacy faced and how successful it was in tackling them. The headings used in the chapter should help you to organise the material. As you make your notes try to decide whether the Confederate government should be praised or blamed for the way it handled things. How good a war leader was Davis? Could the state rights issue have been handled differently? Did Davis's government allow the Confederacy to 'die of democracy'? How might the Confederate government have successfully paid for the war? How successful was the Confederate economy? What impact did the war have on Southerners and could the government have done anything more to ease people's suffering? How serious was the internal opposition?

Source-based questions on 'The Southern Home Front'

1 The Confederate Cabinet
Study the list of Confederate cabinet members on page 65. Answer the following questions.
a) Comment on the number of Secretaries of War (4 marks)
b) According to the cabinet list, which four men would appear to have had most influence over President Davis? What criteria have you used for your selection of the four men? (5 marks)
c) In your opinion which four cabinet members really had most influence over the Confederate war effort? Justify your selection. (6 marks)

2 Inflation
Examine the price statistics from the Richmond Dispatch on page 74. Answer the following questions.
a) To what extent is the Richmond Dispatch likely to be a reliable source of evidence for food prices in Richmond? (5 marks)
b) Which two items seem to have been in particularly short supply by 1863? Explain why this might have been the case. (4 marks)
c) Which two items seem to have been reasonably easy to obtain in 1863? Explain why this might have been the case. (4 marks)
d) What other information is needed for this source to have much use as an indication of 1863 Confederate living standards? (3 marks)
e) What other types of sources might indicate the extent of inflation in Richmond by 1863? (4 marks)

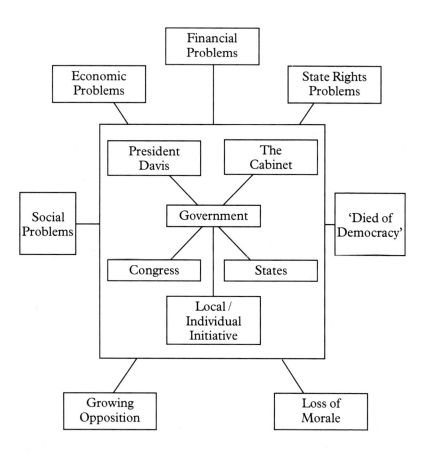

Summary - The Southern Home Front

CHAPTER 5

The Northern Home Front

1 Introduction

The North, with its greater manpower and resources, was always favourite to win the Civil War. However, 'big battalions' do sometimes lose wars. If Northern morale had collapsed, as American morale collapsed during the Vietnam War, the Union could have been defeated. Resources by themselves do not win wars: they need efficient management. Abraham Lincoln was the North's 'top' manager. He was fortunate in that he took over a 'going' concern. But the extent of that concern should not be exaggerated. Before 1861 Americans rarely saw a Federal official, except for the local postmaster, and had little contact with Washington. Lincoln's ability to control matters was limited: he did not head a well-organised and well-directed machine. His administration was heavily dependent on assistance from state governments and voluntary associations. It was also dependent on the Northern economy producing the 'goods'. This chapter will consider how well Lincoln's government rose to the challenge of directing the war effort and what impact the war had on Northern economic and social life. Given that the collapse of Northern morale was the South's best hope of victory, it will also examine the extent to which the North was unified in its war effort.

2 Government in the North

a) Abraham Lincoln

It is difficult to be objective about Lincoln. His assassination in April 1865, just as the Civil War was won, has given him saint-like status. Seen as the saviour of his nation, he is usually regarded as America's greatest President. However, many contemporaries would have been staggered by this opinion - as might Lincoln himself. Many Northerners in the early 1860s saw Lincoln as irresolute and ridiculous. (His ungainly appearance did not help!) His informal western manners inspired little confidence among easterners. Even some of his nearest colleagues doubted his capacity. Throughout the war there was considerable opposition to him, both from the Democrats and from within his own Republican party. So unpopular was Lincoln in the summer of 1864 that it seemed he would not be re-elected President.

It is not difficult to make a case against Lincoln. Before becoming President he had held no significant military command nor any important political position, and he had had little administrative experience. Not surprisingly, he was not to prove a particularly good bureaucrat: his desk was usually cluttered; and his small staff did not

The last photograph of President Lincoln in April 1865

Francis Carpenter's famous painting of Lincoln and his cabinet. The Liberal members are on the left, the conservative on the right. Lincoln is left of centre

provide much assistance. The machinery of government, in consequence, often became clogged. Given that his contact with his main military and government officers was at best sporadic, he was often out of touch. He can also be accused of meddling and incompetence, especially in military matters. Certainly his choice of commanders of the Army of the Potomac down to 1863 - McDowell, McClellan, Pope, McClellan (again), Burnside, and Hooker - did not inspire confidence. Some historians have depicted Lincoln as essentially a devious politician: a man who spent hours each day dealing with corrupt bankers and politicians rather than devoting his time to the war effort. It can be claimed - with much justification - that he deserves little credit for foreign policy (handled by Seward), financial measures (handled by Chase) or economic matters (which were left to Congress).

During the war Lincoln's Democrat opponents accused him of exerting executive tyranny and abusing the constitution. There is some justice in this charge. In September 1862 Lincoln suspended the writ of habeas corpus across the whole of the USA: anyone could be imprisoned by military authority, without recourse to civil courts, for impeding conscription, or affording aid or comfort to the enemy. A horde of petty functionaries could decide, without any clear legal guidelines, precisely who was loyal and who was not. Some, thinking traitors lurked in almost any gathering of Democrats, were overzealous: others simply settled old scores. Altogether, some 40,000 people may have been subject to arbitrary arrest. Unfortunately for his reputation, Lincoln did little to lessen the effects of the harsh measures on individuals. (Given the numbers of people arrested, it would have been difficult for him to have done so!) After the war the Supreme Court condemned the practice of trying civilians by military commissions. In the opinion of some historians, the suppression of civil liberties remains a blot on Lincoln's record.

It is also debatable to what extent Lincoln deserves his reputation as the 'Great Emancipator' (see Chapter 6). At the start of his presidency he moved hesitantly on the slavery issue and seems to have been driven more by practical concerns than conscience. Judged by modern-day standards he was most definitely a racist. He certainly did not regard blacks as equal to whites.

Arguably Lincoln had an easier task than Davis. The North, with its far greater resources, was always favourite to win the Civil War, regardless of who was President. Cynics might claim that it was Lincoln's assassination, rather than his war leadership which assured his reputation.

However, it is far easier to praise Lincoln than to criticise him. Most historians recognise his resilience, his diligence, his tenacity, his honesty (especially in financial matters), his sense of humour, his unassuming style and his deceptive simplicity - and they are right to do so. Lincoln made a profound impression on those he knew him well, not least the members of his own cabinet. The fact that several of his cabinet had far greater experience than their leader (and considered themselves cleverer) did not worry him: he had great self-confidence and no fear of the talents of others. He needed as much talent as he could lay his hands on. Generally, he selected and delegated well, playing his hunches, and giving those men who were successful free reign, even if they despised him. He seems rarely to have despised them.

One of his great fortes was his ability to articulate his - and the Union's - war aims in beautiful writing. Having only a small personal staff - just two secretaries - he wrote his own speeches, unlike most twentieth-century Presidents. The following extract from Lincoln's Annual Message to Congress in December 1862 is a typical example of his eloquence:

1 Fellow-citizens, we cannot escape history. We of this Congress and this administration, will be remembered in spite of ourselves ... The fiery trial through which we pass will light us down in honor or dishonor to the latest generation. We say we are for the Union. The
5 world will not forget that we say this. We know how to save the Union. The world knows we do know how to save it. We, even we here, hold the power and bear the responsibility. In giving freedom to the slave we assure freedom to the free - honorable alike in what we give and what we preserve. We shall nobly save or meanly lose
10 the last, best hope of earth.

Arguably Lincoln's most important role was shaping a national strategy of unconditional surrender, vital to the war's outcome. In some ways he was America's Bismarck - a man of 'blood and iron'. With a mystical faith in the Union, he was determined to fight to the end to preserve it.

Lincoln should be judged by mid-nineteenth-century - not present-day - standards. But his nineteenth-century ideals do help enhance his current reputation. He was, for example, more in favour of racial equality than most Northerners. Throughout his political life he had espoused the Declaration of Independence's view that 'all men are created equal' and as President he was to take up the cause of slavery emancipation (see Chapter 6).

Lincoln was certainly a consummate politician, keeping in touch with public opinion and devoting a remarkable amount of time and energy to matters of patronage and party organisation. As it turned out, this was time well spent. It ensured there were many men within both the Republican party and the government who were loyal to himself, a fact which served him well in 1864. It also helped ensure that the deeply-divided party gave the appearance of unity. One of the ways Lincoln maintained party - and Northern - harmony was to bring into his cabinet all the leading 1860 Republican presidential aspirants who represented the various factions within the party. His man-management skills ensured that he did not really alienate any member of his cabinet.

Lincoln's political skill can be seen in his handling of the crisis of December 1862. By the end of 1862 Northern morale was at a low ebb: the battle of Fredericksburg had been badly handled and many felt there was a need for a drastic shake-up in the administration. In mid-December Republican senators met in caucus to discuss ways of putting new drive into the war. This crisis meeting seems to have been instigated by supporters of Salmon Chase, the radical Secretary of the Treasury. Chase had informed some of the senators that Lincoln's cabinet was divided and that Secretary of State Seward exercised a 'malign influence' on the President. The senators agreed to send delegates to meet Lincoln to demand a vigorous prosecution of the war and cabinet changes, including the ousting of Seward. Lincoln, informed of what was afoot, realised the Senate move was a thinly veiled attack on his own leadership and determined not to lose the considerable talents of Seward. Meeting the delegation of senators in the White House, Lincoln let them present their grievances and make their case against Seward. He then asked them to return the following day. On 19 December he asked all the cabinet members, except Seward, to attend the meeting with the senators. Confronted with his cabinet colleagues, the senators and Lincoln, the embarrassed Chase stated 'that the cabinet were all harmonious' and the bemused senators left. As a result of the crisis both Chase and Seward offered to resign. But Lincoln refused to accept either resignation. He needed Seward (to retain conservative support) and Chase (to keep radical support). The upshot of the crisis was that the cabinet continued as before, with the senators somewhat chagrined, Chase humiliated and Lincoln in a much stronger position.

Lincoln maintained the support of the Republican party throughout the war and he generally worked well with Congress. His views tended to represent the middle ground and he kept open lines of communication with both the radical and conservative wings of his party. Sensitive to the pulse of public opinion, he was always a pragmatist, concerned more with what might be achieved than with what should be achieved. His constant attention to politics, his exquisite sense of political timing and his awareness of what was politically possible, helped the Union to win the war and free the slaves.

Lincoln's main preoccupations throughout his presidency were military matters and race: he rarely focused hard on other problems of policy. There was no need, for example, for him to exert himself on economic matters. The Northern economy was strong and he enjoyed the luxury of a Republican-controlled Congress which enacted the party's economic programme - a programme he fully supported.

As commander-in-chief, Lincoln did not shirk responsibility. Taking the view that waging war was essentially an executive function, he believed he must use his presidential powers to best effect. Where no precedent existed, he was prepared to improvise, stretching the authority of his office beyond any previous practice. He was particularly vigorous in 1861. Before Congress met in July, he alone made the decisions of government. In April 1861, for example, he called for troops, proclaimed a blockade of the South and ordered the spending of $2 million for military and naval measures without Congressional approval. He was also prepared to suspend civil liberties, including both freedom of speech and freedom of the press. In the summer of 1861 he suspended habeas corpus in Maryland, allowing the arrest of suspected Confederates. When Congress finally met, he justified his actions, claiming that in a crisis he had been forced to use his 'war powers' - a new phase. He never defined the limit of these powers but obviously believed they were extensive and throughout the war tried to keep crucial matters under his own control. Inevitably he came into conflict with both Congress and the Supreme Court over the legality of some of his actions. This does not seem to have unduly worried him. His main concern was to win the war. Temporary measures that were deemed necessary to bring about victory, no matter how unprecedented or drastic, were embraced by Lincoln without much agonising over their constitutionality.

Despite some initial insecurity about military matters, he became increasingly involved in the conduct of the war, cajoling, praising and urging his field commanders forward. Before the war he had been a pacific man, if not a pacifist. But some historians think he showed considerable military talent, with an uncanny ability to concentrate on the wider issues rather than becoming bogged down in matters of detail, unlike many of his generals. As early as January 1862 he told two of his generals: 'I state my general idea of this war to be that we have the greater numbers and the enemy has the greater facility of concentrating forces upon points of collision; that we must fail, unless we can find some way of making our advantage an overmatch for his; and that this can only be done by menacing him with superior forces at different points, at the same time'. Unfortunately, and to Lincoln's chagrin, Union generals were unable to carry out such a strategy until 1864-5. Some of Lincoln's appointments were not wise militarily but made sense politically. Appointing generals who represented important ethnic, regional and political constituencies - especially those which had not voted Republican in 1860 - ensured that the North remained united. Ultimately Lincoln's military appointments gave the Union the winning team of Grant and Sherman.

Arguably Lincoln's skilful and vigorous policies in 1861 helped keep the border states in the Union. Although he was ready to use forbearance (for example, respecting Kentucky's neutrality until it was infringed by the Confederacy), he did not shirk from supporting tough measures. In September 1861, for example, he permitted the arrest of a number of men in Maryland's state legislature on the strength of reports that they were about to co-operate with a Confederate invasion scheme.

But military goals rather than political goals were uppermost in the President's mind when he gave the green light to restrict civil liberties. The War Department, which was responsible for military arrests by 1862, was mainly concerned with enforcing conscription. Wholesale military arrests of citizens never happened - not even in enemy areas. Most of those imprisoned without trial came from the South or from states like Missouri which had many Southern sympathisers. Given the grim reality of guerilla war in Missouri, martial law was essential. If the justice dispensed by military commissions in Missouri was rough, so were many of the defendants, who often admitted their, sometimes serious, guilt. Elsewhere moderation was usually the norm. Many of those arrested - Confederate defectors, blockade runners, draft dodgers - would have been arrested whether the writ of habeas corpus had been suspended or not. Moreover those who were arbitrarily arrested usually found themselves being arbitrarily released. Relatively few were brought to - military - trial. Arrests rarely involved Democrat politicians or newspaper editors.

Although Lincoln was prepared to take tough measures, he was far from being a despot. No dictator would have tolerated such fierce opposition in Congress and such bitter criticism in the newspapers or a presidential election in the midst of the war. Although he issued decrees without legislative authority, Lincoln later secured Congressional approval for many of his actions and the judiciary also accepted much of what he did as public necessity. Overall, therefore, Lincoln remained faithful to the spirit, if not always the letter, of the Constitution. Later generations have generally approved - even applauded - the way in which he faced and tackled difficult libertarian issues.

For four years Lincoln stuck at his job. He worked hard - from 7am to 11pm most days - granting favours, issuing pardons, distributing jobs, corresponding with a host of friends, allies and enemies, giving or listening to advice, accepting or rejecting proposals, exerting or responding to pressure. The fact that he had excellent health (he did not drink or smoke) gave him an edge over Jefferson Davis who suffered from numerous - stress-related - illnesses. Lincoln, although often severely depressed, just kept going even when the war was going badly. Nothing kept him from his work - not even his own personal tragedies. (His youngest son died in 1862 and his wife was mentally unstable thereafter.) He learned from his mistakes and revealed real qualities of leadership.

The following extract by Nathanial Hawthorne, a famous writer who met Lincoln in the spring of 1862, provides a good description of the President's appearance and style:

1 There is no describing his lengthy awkwardness nor the
  uncouthness of his movement; and yet it seemed as if I had been in

the habit of seeing him daily, and had shaken hands with him a
thousand times in some village street ... If put to guess his calling
5 and livelihood, I should have taken him for a country schoolmaster
as soon as anything else. He was dressed in a rusty black frock-coat
and pantaloons, unbrushed, and worn so faithfully that the suit
had adapted itself to the curves and angularities of his figure, and
had grown to be an outer skin of the man. He had shabby slippers
10 on his feet. His hair was black, still unmixed with gray, stiff,
somewhat bushy, and had apparently been acquainted with neither
brush nor comb that morning ... His complexion is dark and
sallow ... he has thick black eyebrows and an impending brow, his
nose is large, and the lines about his mouth are very strongly
15 defined. The whole physiognomy is as coarse a one as you would
meet anywhere in the length and breadth of the States; but withal it
is redeemed, illuminated, softened, and brightened by a kindly
though serious look out of his eyes, and an expression of homely
sagacity, that seems weighted with rich results of village
20 experience. A great deal of native sense; no bookish cultivation, no
refinement; honest at heart, and thoroughly so, and yet, in some
sort, sly, - at least, endowed with a sort of tact and wisdom that are
akin to craft, and would impel him, I think, to take an antagonist in
flank, rather than to make a bull-run at him right in front. But on
25 the whole, I like .this sallow, queer, sagacious visage, with the
homely human sympathies that warmed it ... Immediately on his
entrance the President accosted our member of Congress who had
us in charge, and, with a comical twist of his face, made some
jocular remark about the length of his breakfast. He then greeted
30 us all round, not waiting for an introduction, but shaking and
squeezing everybody's hand with the utmost cordiality ... His
manner towards us was wholly without pretense, but yet had a kind
of natural dignity, quite sufficient to keep the forwardest of us from
clapping him on the shoulder and asking him for a story.

b) Lincoln's Cabinet

Lincoln's first cabinet was balanced, containing four ex-Democrats and
three ex-Whigs and a mixture of westerners and easterners. It was more
a cabinet of all the factions than of all the talents. Most of the men had
been challengers to Lincoln for the Republican presidential nomination
in 1860. Influential and experienced politicians, they represented a
variety of factions within the Republican party: factions which needed to
be heard. In 1861 many doubted whether Lincoln would be able to
control such a disparate group. The President soon proved that had the
ability to do so. Despite tensions, jealousies and animosities, Lincoln
knew exactly where he stood with each of his Secretaries. His cabinet
proved to be far more stable than that of Davis, most of the Secretaries

remaining at their posts for most of the war.

In 1861-2 Lincoln bothered little with the cabinet as such: it rarely met formally; and there was no system of collective responsibility. Lincoln used the - rare - meetings as a sounding board to discuss the timing or language of statements he was about to issue or to get approval for actions he was about to take. While he listened to the cabinet's advice, he rarely required its consent. He decided what to do. The Secretaries (some of whom hated each other) simply got on with running their departments, usually seeing the President individually rather than en masse. Within their departments, cabinet members performed well, co-operating when they had to, working hard themselves and keeping their subordinates hard at work.

William Seward, Secretary of State, had been a former governor of New York and a senator for 12 years and thus had far more political and administrative experience than the President. In 1861 he had seen himself playing a sort of prime ministerial role within Lincoln's government. But as he took measure of Lincoln he quickly changed his mind. Seward, who had the reputation of being a radical in 1860, was in reality far more of a conservative. Lincoln valued his advice and Seward was regarded as his right-hand man.

Salmon Chase, Secretary of the Treasury, was the main spokesmen for the anti-slavery, radical wing of the Republican party. An aloof, serious man, he seldom told a joke or could understand one. Although he was sometimes critical of Lincoln and had his own presidential ambitions, Chase was to serve the Union well.

Lincoln's first Secretary of War, Simon Cameron, did not serve so effectively. He had a reputation for corruption before the war and this reputation was not helped by events in 1861-2. As the War Department grew rapidly in size, there were great opportunities for corruption. Cameron, a Pennsylvanian, gave a suspiciously large number of contracts to Pennsylvania firms and military traffic frequently travelled on railways in which he had direct financial interests. He soon became associated with the purchase of 'shoddy' goods. (Shoddy, an inferior wool made from reworked rags, was used by some manufacturers to make uniforms which came apart in the rain: it became the slang term for all inferior goods supplied by government contractors.) To be fair to Cameron, it was inevitable that the rapid build up of the Union army in 1861 would pose administrative problems: the War Department had simply too few experienced bureaucrats. But Cameron's slipshod administrative procedures did not help matters. In 1862 Lincoln sent him as minister to Russia and appointed in his place Edwin Stanton, an ex-Democrat, who proved himself energetic, efficient, decisive and incorruptible, albeit prone to intrigue. 'Don't send me to Stanton to ask a favour,' begged one of Lincoln's private secretaries. 'I would rather make a tour of a smallpox hospital'. Once a severe critic of Lincoln, Stanton became one of his closest advisers.

Montgomery Blair was Postmaster. He came from one of the best-known political families in the North. On the conservative wing of the party, his father continued to own slaves until 1865. Caleb Smith, Secretary of the Interior, played only a minimal role. Bates, the Attorney General, was a conservative ex-Whig from Missouri. Gideon Welles, Secretary of the Navy, was a man of great ability and integrity and served the Union well throughout the war.

c) Congress

Depleted by the loss of its Southern members, Congress was very much controlled by the Republicans. In 1861 the House of Representatives had 105 Republicans, 43 Democrats and 28 'Unionists'. Of the 48 Senators, 31 were Republican. Given the Republican dominance, it is perhaps not surprising that Congress generally co-operated with Lincoln (who maintained close contact with a number of leading Congressmen). Although sometimes bitterly attacked, even by leaders of his own party, Lincoln vetoed only one important bill in four years and, although there was some conflict over the boundaries of executive and legislative power, Congress loyally provided the means for Lincoln to conduct the war.

The 37th Congress, which met in special session in July-August 1861, was probably the most co-operative, ratifiying many of Lincoln's extra-legal actions. The second session of the 37th Congress, which sat from December 1861 to July 1862, was one of the most productive in American history, introducing a number of important economic and fiscal measures, made possible by the absence of Southern Democrats. The 1862 mid-term elections proved to be only a minor setback for the Republicans as the party retained its dominance, albeit diminished, in Congress. The 38th Congress continued to co-operate with Lincoln, although there were some differences on reconstruction policy in 1864.

The Congressional Joint Committee set up in October 1861 to investigate the conduct of the war did pose some problems for Lincoln. Dominated by radicals, it exceeded its brief, investigating many aspects of military policy. Radical Republicans - the most energetic and militant wing of the party - often blamed Lincoln for failing to prosecute the war more vigorously or to move against slavery more rapidly. However, the radicals were not a tight-knit or disciplined group. Nor were they inveterate enemies of Lincoln. When he wanted their support, he usually got it, especially if it was a case of defeating the common Democratic enemy. Indeed in most respects Lincoln and the radicals had similar aims.

d) State Government and Voluntary Associations

Throughout the war, most state governments - controlled by Republican governors and legislatures - provided invaluable assistance to Lincoln, especially in raising and equipping troops. Two Northern states did fall under Democrat control during the war but then did nothing which really hindered the Union war effort. City as well as state government also played an important role. Studies of cities such as Philadelphia indicate that local officials were often remarkably successful in meeting the challenge of war. These studies also indicate the importance of voluntary associations - for example, Church groups and business and trade networks - in the Northern war effort. Neither the Federal nor state governments had the apparatus or traditions to manage all aspects of the war. Voluntary organisations did much to fill the gaps. For example, the United States Sanitary Commission created in 1861 to organise private medical relief, did much to help the Army Medical Bureau. Sanitary Commissioners prowled Union camps and hospitals, insisting on better food and conditions. While the Commission was led by prominent men, thousands of women were the mainstay of the organisation, knitting, wrapping bandages and raising funds.

3 Financing the War

The Union had many advantages over the Confederacy in terms of paying for the conflict. In 1861 it had an established Treasury, gold reserves, land assets and an assured source of revenue from customs duties paid on imported goods. Nevertheless, Northern banking and financial structures were not ready for the conflict, and over the winter of 1861-2 financial problems threatened to overwhelm the Northern cause. In January 1862 the whole Northern banking system seemed near to collapse. 'The bottom is out of the tub,' moaned Lincoln, 'What shall I do?'

The fact that the 1861-2 crisis passed was in part due to the work of Salmon Chase. Chase kept the Treasury afloat in the war's early months by raising short-term loans and issuing bonds, in which ordinary citizens, as well as bankers, were encouraged to invest. Perhaps as many as one million Northerners ended up owning shares in the national debt. Two-thirds of the Union's revenue was raised by loans and bonds. One-fifth was raised by taxes. Chase introduced two new taxes. A Federal income tax, the first in American history, was enacted in August 1861 and imposed a 3 per cent tax on annual incomes over $800. Far more important (it brought in almost ten times as much as the income tax) was the Internal Revenue Act of July 1862 which basically taxed everything and hit the consumer hard.

Congress also approved an inflationary monetary policy. In February

1862 the Legal Tender Act authorised the issuing of $150 million in paper currency, not redeemable in gold or silver. Ultimately 'greenback' notes to the value of $431 million were issued. The Legal Tender Act provided the Treasury with resources to pay its bills and restored investors' confidence sufficiently to make possible the sale of $500 million of new bonds. Inflation did not prove to be ruinous as some economists feared. For the war as a whole the North experienced inflation of only 80 per cent.

Linked to these measures were attempts to reform the banking system. Chase supported the chartering of national banks authorised to issue notes secured by government bonds. His ideas finally bore fruit in the 1863 and 1864 National Banking Acts. These tried to end wildcat banking and establish a sounder and more uniform currency. While the new national banks pumped paper money into the economy, a tax of 10 per cent on state bank notes effectively ensured that the Union was not awash with paper money.

4 The Northern Economy

Before the war Republicans had pressed for the use of Federal funds to advance enterprise and develop America's resources. After 1861 the Republican party was able to pass major economic legislation previously held up by Democrat obstructionism. Some of the legislation was designed to stimulate agriculture. In May 1862 Congress set up a Department of Agriculture which encouraged scientific farming and provided instruction to farmers. In May 1862 the Republicans passed the Homestead Act. Designed to encourage western expansion and open up millions of acres, this offered 160-acre farms free of charge to settlers who worked on them for five years. The July 1862 Morrill Act provided Federal lands to states that built agricultural colleges and colleges for 'the mechanic arts'.

Other legislation aimed to help Northern industry. Higher customs duties not only provided the government with extra revenue but also protected American industry from foreign competition. The inflationary monetary policy, supported by Chase and Congress, also helped industry. The increased money supply ensured that manufacturers found it easier to pay off their debts and to secure loans for investment and expansion. Generous railway subsidies were meted out, not least the granting away of 225 million acres of land to railway companies. The most important railway development was the granting of charters to the Union Pacific and Central Pacific companies in July 1862 to build a line from Omaha to San Francisco, thus ensuring a transcontinental railway.

By twentieth-century standards, however, there was relatively little assertion of Federal power in the management of the wartime economy. Indeed there was far less regulation of the economy in the North than in the South. No elaborate government apparatus was created. There was no rationing; no attempt to control prices, wages and profits; and, while Stanton sometimes leaned on railway bosses, there was no central control of the transportation system. Although the government was now a huge customer, manufacturers made their own decisions and controlled their own production

The economic impact of the war on the North was quite different from its impact on the South. During the war the Confederate states were to experience scarcity and suffer considerable destruction of property. This did not happen in the North. The Northern economy, with its abundant raw materials, technological expertise and ready capital, was able to ensure that Northern armies were well equipped and that Northern civilians did not go short of basic commodities.

It was not certain in 1861 that Northern industry would meet the challenge. The loss of Southern markets, Southern cotton and the repudiation of Southern debts threatened potential disaster. However, the overall effect of the Civil War, especially the need to feed, equip and arm the Union forces, is often seen as stimulating economic growth and prosperity in the North. Production gains were especially notable in war-related industries such as canned food, the boot and shoe industry, shipbuilding, munitions, and iron and steel. For example, iron production was 29 per cent higher in the North in 1864 than it had been for the whole country in the previous record year of 1856. Northern railways, benefiting from the generous subsidies given by the government, made great profits. For the first time their full carrying capacity was utilised.

Northern farmers also benefited from the war. Union forces had to be fed and there was an increased demand from abroad, particularly from Britain which suffered three years of poor harvests in the early 1860s. Exports of wheat, corn, pork and beef doubled. The Northern states grew more wheat in 1862-3 than the USA as a whole had grown in the previous record year of 1859 - and this despite the fact that many farm boys were serving in the Union armies. The growth in production was due in part to the increasing amount of land brought under cultivation - over 2,500,000 acres between 1862 and 1864. But it was also the result of the increased use of farm machinery, especially reapers, mowers and threshers. Between 1860 and 1865 the number of machines on Northern farms increased threefold, while farming in general became more scientific and specialised, with more attention given to crop rotation, fertilisation, animal breeding and drainage. New state Boards of Agriculture, the Federal Department of Agriculture and the handful of agricultural colleges all offered encouragement and instruction in more profitable methods of farming.

But not all economic historians are convinced that the war had a positive effect on the Northern economy. They point out that Northern industry, especially New England cotton mills, suffered hard times in the first year of the war. The fact that so much of the labour force was drawn into the armed services may have slowed down industrial and agricultural production. Moreover, the growth of population by immigration was severely curtailed. The war may have reduced immigration by some 1,300,000 people - nearly twice the number lost by both sides in the war. According to some estimates, the combined effect of loss in immigration and military deaths reduced the population by 5.6 per cent from what it would have been without the war. Economic growth in the North in the 1860s was slower (it is claimed) than in any other decade in the nineteenth century. If there was a shift to mass production, this was arguably a trend that was well under way before the Civil War and one that was not particularly affected by it.

The war undoubtedly had some damaging effects on the North, particularly in 1861-2. But it is also true that the Northern economy grew, in spite - or because - of the war. The North had no difficulty maintaining its vast forces. In March 1865 one newspaper reported: 'There never was a time in the history of New York when business prosperity was more general, when the demand for goods was greater ... than within the last two or three years'. According to historian Peter Parish, 'The abiding impression [of the Northern economy] is one of energy and enterprise, resilience and resource ... The war was not the soil in which industrial growth took root, nor a blight which stunted it, but a very effective fertiliser'.

5 The Impact of the War on Northern Society

In many ways life for most Northerners during the war went on as usual. However, as in the South, the fact that Union regiments were often made up of men from a single town or county could mean sudden calamity for a neighbourhood if that regiment suffered 50 per cent (or more) casualties in a single battle - as many did.

The fact that so many men of military age left their homes to fight (50 per cent in most Western states) enlarged the social and economic role of women on most farms. The war also created new job opportunities for women - as teachers, nurses, and in industry and state or Federal government service. However, despite the high expectations of women's rights advocates, the war did not bring women significantly closer to political or economic equality.

Some historians think the war may have led to increased social and economic tension. There is some evidence that during the war the rich became richer while the poor became poorer. For some groups the war certainly resulted in economic hardship. Many Northern working men saw their real earnings drop as prices rose faster than wages. The result was increased labour unrest and some violent strikes, especially in 1863-4. However, these were generally small-scale affairs. Small firms remained the norm and there was little to be gained by workers in family businesses downing tools. Moreover, some workers benefited from increased wages resulting from a shortage of labour. Many working-class families also benefited from bounties and wages paid to soldiers who, between them, sent millions of dollars home. Overall, therefore, it is difficult to claim that there was a great increase in class tension.

In some parts of the North the war led to an increase in racial tensions. Some Northerners, fearing the results of emancipation and the possibility of ex-slaves pouring northwards, resented fighting a war to free the slaves. Anti-black feeling was also fanned by job competition and the employment of black strikebreakers. In 1863 there were violent race riots in a number of northern cities - Chicago, Detroit, Cleveland, Buffalo, and Boston. The most serious was in New York (see below). However, the war does seem to have had positive effects for many Northern black Americans. Most seem to have felt a sense of increased racial pride and many looked forward with optimism to the future.

Immigration had been an important social - and political - issue before the war. In the short term, the war led to a reduction in immigrant numbers; for example, 92,000 in 1861-2 compared with 154,000 in 1860. But this state of affairs did not last long. In 1863 there were over 176,000 immigrants and by 1865 nearly 250,000 - proof of the North's booming war economy and also of the government's success in publicising opportunities and encouraging immigrants. Many immigrants, attracted by the high bounties, volunteered for the Union army. Others, by filling key jobs, helped the Northern economy. The war may have helped the process of assimilation and possibly tamed the nativism (anti-immigrant feeling) of the 1850s. Most Northerners seem to have welcomed (even Irish Catholic) immigrants who could help the war effort.

6 Opposition to the War

The vast majority of Northerners were determined to preserve the Union and fully supported the war effort. In 1861 leading Northern Democrats like Senator Douglas called on all Northerners to rally round Lincoln. Most Northern Democrats supported the call for troops and the measures to sustain them. Lincoln, aware of the importance of retaining the support of all Northerners, promoted ex-Democrats to his cabinet and gave high military appointments to men whom he knew were political opponents. Some Democrats (they are usually called War Democrats) threw in their lot totally with Lincoln and effectively became Republicans.

But as the war progressed, Democrat opposition to many of Lincoln's measures increased. Many Democrats were critical of the way the war was being handled. They also opposed Republican economic policies, conscription and (what they perceived to be) Lincoln's arbitrary measures. They insisted that the war should not be waged to subjugate the South and opposed all measures that proposed an end to slavery.

Reflecting and exploiting Northern racist views for all they were worth and capitalising on growing war weariness, the Democrats had some success in the mid-term elections of 1862. Their 1862 slogan was: 'The Constitution as it is: the Union as it was: the Negroes where they are'.

Although Democrats increasingly saw the conflict as a Republican war, most still wanted to restore the Union: pro-Confederate Northerners were a very small minority. This was not the way that many Republicans saw it. Worried at the growing opposition, Republicans began to claim that leading Democrats were at best faint-hearted appeasers and at worst traitors. In the West, Republicans labelled their Democratic opponents 'Copperheads'. (A copperhead was a poisonous snake.) After Democrat victories in the autumn 1862 elections, Republicans intensified their smear campaign, often now referring to the Democrat party as the Copperhead party. Some Republicans went further and claimed that the Copperheads belonged to subversive, pro-Southern secret societies like the Knights of the Golden Circle or the Sons of Liberty. In the fevered imaginations of some radical Republicans, these organisations had massive membership and planned to set up a 'Northwest Confederacy' which would split from the Union and make peace with the South. Republican leaders realised that charges of treason and sedition could be used to discredit the Democrat party as a whole and could serve as an excuse to organise Union Leagues - Republican-led patriotic societies pledged to defend the Union. The Union Leagues soon exerted much greater influence than the Democratic organisations.

Democrat dissent probably reached its height in the first half of 1863 when Union military failures fostered a sense of defeatism. Some Democrats suggested that the war was unconstitutional, could not be won and that the time had come to make peace with the Confederacy. A few tried to discourage enlistment, aware that in so doing they were courting arrest. (In September 1862 Lincoln had suspended the writ of habeas corpus to permit the arrest of 'all Rebels and Insurgents, their aiders and abettors within the United States, and all persons discouraging volunteer enlistments, resisting militia drafts, or guilty of any disloyal practice'.) One of the leading peace Democrats was Clement Vallandigham. In the spring of 1863, hoping to be elected governor of Ohio, Vallandigham publicly denounced the war and called upon soldiers to desert. Vallandigham was deliberately seeking martyrdom and a martyrdom of sorts duly followed. In May 1863, on the orders of General Burnside (whose political finesse was no more subtle that his military judgement), Vallandigham was arrested at his house in the middle of the night. Tried by a military tribunal, he was found guilty of treason and sentenced to imprisonment for the rest of the war.

Vallandigham's treatment led to a chorus of protest from outraged Democrats. Even some Republicans were appalled that a civilian had been tried and sentenced by a military court merely for making a speech. Lincoln did not much like what Burnside had done but saw no alternative but to support him. Vallandigham, by discouraging enlistment and encouraging desertion, had clearly broken the law and the suspension of habeas corpus in his case seemed fair. 'Must I shoot a simple-minded soldier-boy who deserts, while I must not touch a hair of a wiley agitator who induces him to desert?,' mused Lincoln. 'I think that in such a case, to silence the agitator, and save the boy is not only constitutional, but withal a great mercy'. However, Lincoln was anxious to avoid making Vallandigham a martyr. In the end he decided to free him but also - and this was an effective move - to banish him to the Confederacy for the duration of the war. Vallandigham, soon tiring of the South, moved to Canada where he continued to conduct his campaign for governor of Ohio. But the upturn in Union military fortunes after July 1863 undermined his peace platform and his political ambitions were easily thwarted. Other pro-peace Democratic candidates also lost election contests in 1863.

The most serious internal violence in the North came in New York in July 1863. The New York riots followed the enforcement of a Conscription Act in the summer of 1863. By the terms of the Act (passed in March 1863), all men between the ages of 20 and 45 could be enrolled in the armed forces for three years. However, any man who was prepared to pay $300 (a year's wages for an unskilled labourer) or find a substitute was exempt. Given the slump in recruitment, the Act was probably necessary. But it was one of the most divisive issues of the war. Denouncing it as an unconstitutional measure to achieve an unconstitutional end (the freeing of the slaves), Democrats in Congress voted against it. Many disliked the fact that it seemed to favour the wealthy: the view that this was a 'rich man's war and a poor man's fight' was not confined to the South. The Act sparked off draft riots in many Northern cities but the bloodiest was in New York.

New York's Democrat Governor, Horatio Seymour had been whipping up opposition to the draft for weeks. When the names of the first draftees were drawn, a mob of mostly Irish workers attacked and destroyed the recruiting station. The mob them went on the rampage, venting its fury on free blacks who were blamed for the war. (Some had been used as strike-breakers in a number of recent strikes.) A few blacks were lynched and for several days New York was in chaos. Economic grievances were in part responsible for the riots but ethnic, racial and religious factors also played a part. Whatever the main causes of the riots (which historians continue to debate), the situation obviously posed a major challenge to the authority of Lincoln's administration. The President moved quickly, sending in 20,000 troops. Fresh from their victory at Gettysburg, the soldiers swiftly restored order. At least 120 people (and possibly many more) died. Most of the dead were rioters shot by the troops.

7 Conclusion

The New York riots and the strong Democrat opposition are useful reminders that the Union was far from united. Not all Northerners viewed Lincoln's leadership as positively as most historians have done. Unappreciated by many of his countrymen during the war, Lincoln was often blamed when things went wrong. But for the most part opposition to both Lincoln and the war was expressed legally within the political structures. Many historians are convinced that the existence of a responsible, disciplined and for the most part loyal opposition - which helped keep dissent within limits - helped to unify the Northern war effort and made a significant contribution to Northern victory. Democrat criticism could also be constructive: it helped keep the government 'honest'; and it played a legitimate and important role in keeping the issue of civil liberties in the public eye. Finally, Democrat opposition led to heightened co-operation between Republicans in Congress and helped nurture a relationship of mutual support between Republican state officials and Lincoln's administration.

Lincoln did provide strong leadership. But he was no superman. He was always ready to admit that events controlled him rather than he controlled events. His administration did relatively little to manage the economic resources which ultimately produced victory. In a sense the Northern economy ran itself. Fortunately for Lincoln, Northern factories were able to meet all the needs of war - and more. After 1863 the Northern economy boomed. The fact that the Union was able to produce both 'guns' and 'butter' helped Northern morale. Most Northerners supported Lincoln and determined to see the war to a victorious conclusion.

Making notes on 'The Northern Home Front'

Your notes on this chapter and the last should give you an understanding of the problems faced by both sides in managing the war effort on the home front, enabling you to assess the leadership qualities of Lincoln and Davis and the strength of opposition they faced. Was the Northern war effort more - or less - 'total' than that of the South? Your notes should also provide you with a view on whether the war impeded or enhanced the North's social and economic development.

Answering essay questions on 'The Northern Home Front'

It is likely you will use information from the last two chapters to answer questions which ask you to compare North and South. Consider the following questions:

1 Assess the presidential talents of Abraham Lincoln and Jefferson Davis. Who proved himself to be the better leader?
2 Account for the internal opposition to both Lincoln and Davis in the Civil War?

Question 1 seems straightforward. But be warned! It is deceptively easy to write a narrative, all-I-know-about answer, starting with Lincoln and finishing with Davis - with a last sentence saying something like: 'Thus Lincoln proved himself to be the better leader'. Such answers often score low marks. The key word in the question is 'Assess'. This means you are being asked to make judgements about both Lincoln and Davis. First-class answers invariably consider the criteria by which Lincoln and Davis are to be judged. They then go on to examine the extent to which the two Presidents met these criteria. It is worth compiling a list of seven or eight criteria by which you might wish to adjudge Lincoln and Davis's performance. This list should provide a good framework for an essay plan. But remember you are also specifically asked to decide who was the better leader. The answer to this question might seem self-evident: Lincoln led the winning side while Davis was defeated. Enough said! (It will be as much as many students say!) But really good answers will be more subtle. They will consider Northern advantages and Southern weaknesses. Was Lincoln's job easier than that of Davis? Could (almost) anyone have led the North to victory? To what extent did Davis's strong leadership ensure that the Confederacy survived as long as it did? At the end of the day you might well decide (as I think I might!) that Lincoln was the better leader. But at least you will have engaged in debate. And remember that examiners are often very impressed by candidates who can present an effective argument, supported by hard evidence, that casts doubt on usual assumptions.

Question 2 does not ask you to write all you know about the opposition to Lincoln and Davis but rather to 'account' for that opposition. Draw up a rough plan for this question and also write both an introductory and a concluding paragraph.

Source-based questions on 'The Northern Home Front'

1 Lincoln's War Aims
Read the extract from Lincoln's 1862 speech on page 88 and the Gettysburg Address on page 58. Answer the following questions.
a) What seem to be Lincoln's main war aims? (4 marks)
b) What did Lincoln mean in the phrase, 'The last best hope of earth'? (3 marks)
c) Comment on Lincoln's spoken and written style as presented in the two extracts. (8 marks)

2 President Lincoln

Examine the photograph and Carpenter's painting, and read Hawthorne's description of Lincoln on pages 86 and 91-2. Answer the following questions.

a) What are the strengths and weaknesses of the photograph, the painting, and the written description in giving us an honest 'picture' of 'Honest Abe'!? (15 marks)

b) What does Hawthorne's account tell us of Lincoln's presidential 'style'? (5 marks)

c) Hawthorne's description of his meeting with Lincoln so offended the editor of the journal for which he was writing that large sections of it were not printed. Why do you think this was? (5 marks)

d) Comment on Lincoln's position in Carpenter's painting. (5 marks)

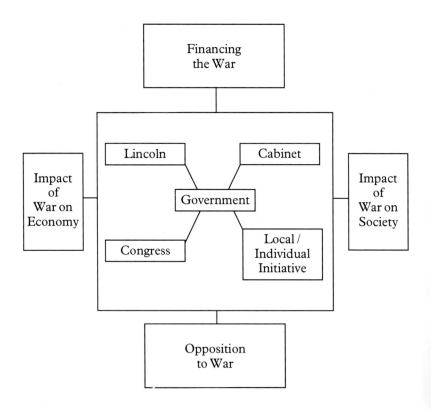

Summary - The Northern Home Front

CHAPTER 6

The Destruction of Slavery

1 The Situation in 1861

In 1861 the black abolitionist leader Frederick Douglass predicted: 'The American people and the Government of Washington may refuse to recognise it for a time but the inexorable logic of events will force it upon them in the end; that the war now being waged in this land is a war for and against slavery'. However, only slowly did the war to save the Union become a war to free the slave. From start to finish most Northern Democrats fought simply to restore the Union and opposed freeing slaves. In 1861 most Republicans were also reluctant to support emancipation as an overt war aim. There was strong racial prejudice in the North. Many Northerners feared that freed slaves might move North, with disastrous effects. President Lincoln was aware of the importance of preserving Northern unity. An avowed policy of freeing the slaves would certainly alienate the four slave states which remained within the Union - Kentucky, Maryland, Missouri and Delaware - which together had some 400,000 slaves. It was also likely to spur Southerners to greater efforts and leave no possibility for a compromise peace.

In consequence, to the dismay of abolitionists like Douglass, both Lincoln and Congress tackled the slavery issue with great caution in the first months of the war. In April 1861, Lincoln sent a letter to the representatives of the Virginia secession convention in which he declared:

I have no purpose, directly or indirectly, to interfere with the institution of slavery in the States where it exists. I believe I have no lawful right to do so, and I have no inclination to do so.

Lincoln made it clear that he was willing to put off any definitive action on emancipation, in order to keep open the option of negotiating a settlement with the Confederacy. Congress supported this stance. In July 1861 the Crittenden resolution, which disclaimed any intention of meddling with 'the rights or established institutions' of the South, won overwhelming approval in both the Senate and the House of Representatives. In the summer of 1861 the Northern goal was the speedy restoration of the Union under the Constitution and the laws of 1861, all of which recognised the legitimacy of slavery.

2 Pressures for Emancipation 1861-2

As the months went by and it became increasingly clear that there was little likelihood of the Confederate states being enticed back into the Union, different views began to prevail. Radical Republicans began to make their influence felt. Most radicals believed that to fight slaveholders without fighting against slavery, was (in Douglass's words) 'a half-hearted business'. They wanted to abolish slavery and create a new order in the South.

Radical Republicans had a variety of motives. All were opposed to slavery. Some, but not all, were genuinely concerned for black Americans. Most, if not all, had a loathing of white slaveholders who they blamed for causing the war. There was a general concern that if the Union was restored without slavery being abolished, nothing would have been solved. Radicals, almost without exception, believed that measures to emancipate slaves would weaken the Southern war effort. Finally, if emancipation became a Northern war aim there was little chance that Britain or France would support the Confederacy. 'It is often said that war will make an end of Slavery,' said Charles Sumner in October 1861. 'This is probable. But it is surer still that the overthrow of Slavery will make an end of the war'.

By the time Congress met again in December 1861, most Republican Congressmen supported a tougher stand against slavery. The House of Representatives now refused to reaffirm Crittenden's resolution and the Senate did not even discuss it. To one Congressman it seemed a powerful faction was already forming whose watchword was 'Emancipation - the utter extinction of slavery'.

A set of forces placed increasing pressure on the Federal government to take some decisive action with regard to emancipation. The most pressing problem was what to do with refugee slaves who came to the camps of Northern armies occupying areas of the Confederacy. By the letter of the Fugitive Slave Law, the slaves should have been returned to their owners and in 1861-2 some Northern soldiers did just that. However, others, on both humane and pragmatic grounds - the slaves would obviously be punished and would also help the Confederate war effort - opposed such action. Army commanders, therefore, played a prominent role in determining policy on emancipation, ahead of the President and Congress. Lincoln tried to evade the whole question, ordering his generals not to allow fugitives within their lines in the first place. But this did not stop slaves fleeing.

In May 1861 General Benjamin Butler hit upon a practical solution. He declared that all slaves who came to his camp were to be confiscated as 'contraband of war', thus ensuring they were not returned to their Confederate owners. This designation neatly avoided the question of whether or not the fugitives were free and turned the Southerners' argument that slaves were property against them. Butler's action was subsequently supported both by Lincoln and by the terms of the Confiscation Act (August 1861). This Act threatened any property used 'for insurrectionary purposes' with confiscation. The Act left unsettled the issue of whether or not such 'confiscated' slaves became free. Even so, it went too far for Democrat Congressmen. All but three voted against it. All but six Republicans voted for it.

In August 1861 General John Frémont, the 1856 Republican presidential candidate and now Federal commander in Missouri, issued a proclamation freeing the slaves of all Confederate activists in Missouri. In Lincoln's view this was a step too far and he requested that Fremont rescind his order. When Frémont refused, Lincoln - to the dismay of the radicals - publicly ordered Fremont to modify his proclamation. Fremont, an inefficient commander as well as a political embarrassment, was soon removed from his Missouri command.

This letter to Senator Browning gives some indication of Lincoln's thinking in the summer of 1861:

1 Frémont's proclamation ... is purely political, and not within the range of military law, or necessity. If a commanding General finds a necessity to seize the farm of a private owner, for a pasture, an encampment, or a fortification, he has the right to do so, and to so 5 hold it, as long as the necessity lasts; and this is within military law, because within military necessity. But to say the farm shall no longer belong to the owner, or his heirs forever ... is purely political, without the savor of military law about it. And the same is true of slaves. If the General needs them, he can seize them, and 10 use them; but when the need is past, it is not for him to fix their permanent future condition. That must be settled according to laws made by law-makers, and not by military proclamations ... I cannot assume this reckless position; nor allow others to assume it on my responsibility. You speak of it as being the only means of 15 saving the government. On the contrary it is itself the surrender of the government.

Radicals increasingly implored Lincoln to declare his support for emancipation. But Lincoln remained hesitant. He had no wish to offend the radicals. He referred to men like Sumner as the conscience of the Republican party and shared the radical conviction that slavery was a moral evil which mocked the Declaration of Independence. He also accepted that he could exercise his war-powers as President and take action against slavery as a military necessity. However, Lincoln had still no wish to alienate conservative Republicans and Northern Democrats and remained concerned about the Union border states which preserved slavery. He thought that if emancipation became a Northern war aim half the officers in his army 'would fling down their arms and three more states would rise'. He also feared that a declaration in favour in emancipation would result in the war degenerating into a 'violent and remorseless struggle'. 'We didn't go to war to put down slavery - but to put the flag back', declared Lincoln, in his annual message to Congress in December 1861: '… the thunderbolt will keep'.

Radical Republicans continued to press for more anti-slavery measures and in the spring of 1862 Congress began to take action. In March 1862 it forbade soldiers to return fugitive slaves to the South. Although this freed no slaves, it did encourage slaves to flee to Union lines. In April 1862 Congress passed a bill abolishing slavery in the District of Columbia: provision was made to compensate slave owners and to support the colonisation of ex-slaves in Liberia or Haiti. In June Congress, voting on straight party lines, abolished slavery in all Federal territories. The following month Congress enacted a second and much more sweeping Confiscation - and Militia - Bill. This allowed the seizure of all 'enemies' property': slaves in such cases were to be set 'forever free'. Lincoln also received Congressional authority to employ 'persons of African descent' in any capacity deemed necessary and proper for the suppression of the rebellion. As a sweetener to Lincoln, Congress again set aside $500,000 for colonisation expenses. The Bill met with considerable resistance in Congress. Some thought it went too far. Others thought it didn't go far enough and were disappointed that the measure proposed to do nothing about slavery in the Union slave states. Lincoln had doubts about the Bill but in the end signed it. In fact, the second Confiscation Act was not as radical as it seemed. The only way that a slave could actually gain freedom was on a case-by-case basis before a Federal court: this court had to find that the slave owner was, in fact, a rebel. Lincoln also interpreted the Militia Act narrowly, permitting the employment of 'contraband' only as army labourers, not real soldiers.

3 Lincoln's Views: Spring/Summer 1862

In July 1862 the abolitionist Garrison described Lincoln's handling of the slavery issue as, 'Stumbling, halting, prevaricating, irresolute, weak, besotted'. He went on to say that the President was 'nothing better than a wet rag'. Many radical Republicans agreed. At best Lincoln had so far followed Northern opinion on the question of slavery. Others - including both Congressmen and army officers - had led it. However, by mid-1862 the President was convinced that some bolder step was necessary. He had already assured the radical Sumner that the only difference between them on the slavery issue was a few weeks. Determined to keep control of the issue, Lincoln thought it was his responsibility to make the final decision on if and when emancipation was essential to the maintenance of the Union.

Even before the summer of 1862, Lincoln had begun to take action. In March 1862 he sent to Congress a request that financial compensation be given to any state which adopted the principle of gradual abolition of slavery. Owners would be given $400 for every slave freed. Hoping that the border states would adopt their own emancipation laws without Federal coercion, he envisaged that the Union slave states would gradually remove slavery over the next 30 years. If the border states began the process, he hoped that some of the rebel states might be persuaded to follow suit. Abolitionists denounced Lincoln's measure, arguing that justice would be better served by compensating the slaves for their long years in bondage than by indemnifying slaveholders for their often grudging loyalty to the Union. Despite opposition from both radicals and conservatives, Congress approved the scheme for gradual compensated emancipation. However, to Lincoln's great disappointment, the border states refused to implement emancipation on any terms.

Thwarted in the North, Lincoln by the summer of 1862, was prepared to act in the South. The situation had changed since 1861. The allegiance of the border states was now reasonably secure. He was aware of the increasing pressure from radicals within his own party and reluctant to alienate so powerful an element. He was also concerned that the image of the USA abroad was tarnished by its failure to act on the slavery issue. His main belief, however, was his conviction that a bold statement on emancipation would weaken the Confederacy. Military necessity dominated his thoughts in the depressing summer of 1862. There was also another issue. Lincoln was concerned that if the Union won, and the Southern states re-entered the Union with the peculiar institution untouched, slavery would still be a source of future strife. The war and blood-letting would have solved nothing.

He revealed his decision to issue an Emancipation Proclamation to Seward and Welles in mid-July. A few days later (22 July) he presented his preliminary Emancipation Proclamation to the entire cabinet. Many of its members greeted the news with astonishment. 'The measure goes beyond anything I have recommended,' said Stanton. Neverthless, all except Blair - who feared that the Proclamation would harm Republican chances in the autumn mid-term elections - approved. However, Seward recommended that the Proclamation should be issued only after a military success; otherwise it would seem like 'the last shriek on our retreat' - an act of desperation born of weakness. Lincoln accepted the logic of this and waited patiently, keeping his intention secret from all but his cabinet. When Horace Greeley wrote a bitter editorial, 'The Prayer of Twenty Millions', criticising the president for not doing more on the slavery front, Lincoln still did not reveal his intentions. He responded to Greeley by saying:

> If I could save the Union without freeing any slave I would do so and if I could save it by freeing all the slaves I would do it; and if I could save it by freeing some and leaving others alone I would also do that.

In early September, Lincoln, in debate with some Chicago Christian ministers, said:

1 I admit that slavery is the root of the rebellion ... I would also concede that emancipation would help us in Europe, and convince them that we are incited by something more than ambition. I grant further that it would help somewhat at the North, though not so 5 much, I fear, as you and those you represent imagine ... And then unquestionably it would weaken the rebels by drawing off their labourers, which is of great importance. But I am not sure we could do much with the blacks. If we were to arm them, I fear that in a few weeks the arms would be in the hands of the rebels ... I will 10 mention another thing, though it meet only your scorn and contempt. There are fifty thousand bayonets in the Union armies from the Border Slave States. It would be a serious matter if, in consequence of a proclamation such as you desire, they should go over to the rebels. I do not think they all would - not so many 15 indeed as a year ago, or as six months ago - not so many today as yesterday ... Let me say one thing more. I think you should admit that we already have an important principle to rally and unite the people in the fact that constitutional government is at stake. This is a fundamental idea, going down about as deep as anything.

4 The Emancipation Proclamation

After the battle of Antietam (a drawn battle which he chose to regard as a victory!), Lincoln decided to act. On 22 September he read to his cabinet his prepared statement on emancipation. He was not, he told his cabinet colleagues, interested in their advice 'about the main matter - for that I have determined for myself'. He asked only for their opinion as to the wisdom of releasing the statement. The cabinet unanimously agreed with Lincoln's draft. Next day details of Lincoln's Emancipation Proclamation were released in newspapers across the USA.

On the surface the Proclamation, justified by Lincoln as 'a fit and necessary war measure', seemed to be extremely cautious. Slavery was to be left untouched in states that returned to the Union before January 1863. Thereafter all slaves in enemy territory conquered by Union armies would be 'forever free'. The Proclamation had no effect whatsoever on slavery in the Union slave states. It did not even effect slavery in those parts of Louisiana, Virginia and Tennessee which had already been brought back under Union control. Indeed in September 1862, the Proclamation liberated not a single slave. The British Prime Minister Palmerston was unimpressed: 'It is not easy to estimate how utterly powerless and contemptible a government must have become which could sanction such trash'. The London *Spectator* said the principle behind the proclamation seemed to be, 'not that a human being cannot justly own another, but that he cannot own him unless he is loyal to the United States'.

However, most abolitionists and radical Republicans were delighted at what they saw as a bold act on Lincoln's part. 'God bless Abraham Lincoln,' wrote Greeley. The war, wrote Douglass was now 'invested with sanctity'. Radicals appreciated that Lincoln had gone as far as his powers allowed in making the war a war to end slavery. Radicals also appreciated that the Emancipation Proclamation added an important moral dimension to the conflict. As Union forces advanced, slavery in the South would end. Once slavery had ended in the South, it could not possibly survive in the border states. At one stroke, Lincoln had turned the war into a revolution.

Northern Democrats saw it this way, disliked what they saw, and vehemently denounced the Proclamation. Aware of the fear of a migration of ex-slaves northwards, Democrats made the Emancipation Proclamation a central issue in the mid-term elections in autumn 1862. Historians once claimed that these elections were a clear triumph for the Democrats, and thus proof that most Northerners were opposed to emancipation. The Republicans lost control of New York, Pennsylvania, Ohio, Indiana and Illinois, and also lost 35 Congressional seats. Even Lincoln acknowledged that his Proclamation contributed to the setbacks. However, on closer analysis, the mid-term election results suggest that the Emancipation Proclamation, only one of many issues in the election, had less impact than Lincoln believed. Overall the Republicans retained control of most free state governorships, kept control of the House of Representatives and gained five seats in the Senate. Democrat majorities in Pennsylvania, Ohio, New York and Indiana were very small and could be explained by the inability of Republican-voting soldiers to vote.

As 1 January 1863 approached some Northerners wondered whether Lincoln would fulfil his promise. He hardly mentioned the Emancipation Proclamation in his annual message to Congress in December 1862. Instead he concentrated on recommending that the Constitution be amended to permit congressional remuneration of all states that abolished slavery at any time pre-1900, or provided for the voluntary colonisation of free African Americans outside the USA. However, there was never any possibility of Lincoln not going through with his emancipation measure. In private he said he would rather die than take back a word of the 'Proclamation of Freedom'. Accordingly on 1 January 1863, Lincoln proclaimed that the freedom of all slaves in rebellious regions was now a Union war aim - 'an act of justice' as well as 'military necessity'. Not wishing to be held responsible for a bloody slave revolt, he urged slaves 'to abstain from all violence, unless in necessary self-defence'. But at the same time, he called on Union forces to protect the rights of those they made free.

Lincoln appreciated that his Proclamation was little more than getting a foot in the emancipation door. But he was confident that once the foot was in the door, it could easily be opened all the way. The Proclamation promised - or as the South saw it threatened - great things. Davis condemned it as 'the most execrable measure recorded in the history of guilty man'. The Confederacy could no longer look for a compromise settlement. If it was going to protect its peculiar institution, it must fight to the bitter end. Lincoln had deliberately raised the stakes of the war. His action was to have a profound effect on the nature and the result of the conflict.

In the short term, the Emancipation Proclamation may well have helped to stiffen Confederate resistance, as Lincoln had feared. (Some Southerners were so outraged by it that they talked of putting captured Union soldiers to death because they now came south with the intent of inciting rebellion!) However, in the long term, the Confederacy was undoubtedly weakened by Lincoln's emancipation policy. The Confederacy now stood little chance of winning foreign, particularly British, support. By encouraging slaves to flee to Union lines, it worsened the South's already serious manpower shortage. As Lincoln said: 'Freedom has given us the control of 200,000 able bodied men, born and raised on southern soil. It will give us more yet. Just so much has it subtracted from the strength of our enemies'.

Only once after September 1862 did Lincoln falter in his commitment to emancipation. In the summer of 1864, as the war dragged on and he seemed to face the prospect of defeat in the presidential election, he possibly considered dropping emancipation as a precondition of peace negotiations. But if he did waver - and there is considerable doubt about this - it was only for a few hours.

5 The African American War Effort

From the start of the war Lincoln had faced strong and conflicting pressure on the question of whether or not to enlist blacks in the Union army. Initially most Northerners, hating the notion of blacks fighting with and against other whites and doubting that blacks would make good soldiers, opposed black recruitment. Black leaders and abolitionists, however, were anxious that blacks should fight in a war that was likely to weaken if not destroy slavery. Pointing out that blacks were serving in the Union navy, they pushed for similar enlistment of black soldiers. 'This is no time to fight with one hand, when both are needed,' declared Douglass: 'this is no time to fight with your white hand and allow your black hand to remain tied'.

Lincoln, unwilling to alienate the Union slave states, stood firm against black recruitment for the first year of the war. This did not prevent some Northerners doing their best to recruit black soldiers. General David Hunter, for example, raised a regiment of black volunteers on the Sea Islands off the coast of South Carolina in the spring of 1862. But Hunter received no financial support from the War Department and was forced to disband his regiment. The July 1862 Confiscation Act gave Lincoln the power to arm 'contraband' ex-slaves and use them as a military force 'for which they may be found competent'. But Lincoln interpreted this narrowly and insisted that ex-slaves should simply be employed as army labourers, not front-line troops. But others in Lincoln's cabinet felt differently. In August 1862 Secretary of War Stanton authorised the creation of a regiment of 5,000 black troops to be recruited in Union-occupied areas of Louisiana. Lincoln did not object and in September the first official regiment of free blacks was mustered into Union service.

After the Emancipation Proclamation, Lincoln's resistance to enlisting black soldiers abated and from spring 1863 onwards there was a large influx of black troops into the Union army. As in so many respects, the President was in tune with Northern public opinion. As casualty lists mounted and white recruitment fell off, Lincoln knew there was far more support for black soldiers than there had been in 1861.

Of the 46,000 free blacks of military age in the North, some 33,000 joined the Union armies. The majority of black troops, however, were ex-slaves. Some 100,000 were recruited from the Confederacy. Another 42,000 slaves from Kentucky, Delaware, Maryland and Missouri also enlisted in the Union army. (This was the swiftest way for border state slaves to get their freedom.) By the summer of 1863 over 30 black regiments had been recruited, under the control of the Bureau for Colored Troops. By October 1864 this number had grown to 140 regiments. By 1865 some 180,000 blacks had served in the Union armies, nearly 10 per cent of the Union total.

At first black troops tended to be assigned to duties behind the fighting line. But as 1863 progressed more black soldiers saw action. In June 1863 black troops acquitted themselves well in an engagement at Milliken's Bend, Louisiana. In July the all-black 54th Massachusetts regiment suffered 40 per cent casualties in an assault on Fort Wagner. Many black regiments took part in the 1864-5 fighting around Petersburg. Most seem to have fought as well as white regiments.

However, within the Union army there was considerable racial discrimination. Many Northern whites disliked the idea of fighting with blacks and regiments were strictly segregated. Black regiments were invariably commanded by white officers. By 1865 scarcely 100 black soldiers had become officers and there were none above the rank of captain. Black regiments had fewer doctors and often received inferior supplies and equipment. What rankled most, however, was the fact that there were pay differentials: white privates received $13 a month while blacks were paid only $10. In November 1863 some black troops protested about their unequal pay. This protest was seen as 'mutiny'. The black sergeant leading the 'mutiny' was found guilty of treason and executed. Although Secretary of War Stanton was sympathetic to black claims for equal treatment, Lincoln was not convinced. Blacks, he thought, had 'larger motives for being soldiers than white men ... they ought to be willing to enter the service upon any condition'. In June 1864, however, Congress at last provided equal pay for black soldiers.

Black troops were in greater danger than whites if they were taken prisoner. Some Confederates boasted that they took no black prisoners and certainly there were occasions when black troops were killed as they tried to surrender (e.g. at Fort Pillow, Tennessee in April 1864). More often black prisoners were returned to slavery. Given that the Confederacy was not prepared to exchange black soldiers, Lincoln stopped all prisoner-of-war exchanges in 1863. This had a more damaging effect on the Confederate war effort than it did on the Union side. It was difficult for Lincoln to respond to the slaughter of black soldiers who tried to surrender. To threaten retaliation would simply lead to further bloodshed by both sides. However, it soon became apparent that Confederate atrocities were a double-edged weapon. The fact that blacks feared maltreatment may have encouraged them to fight to the death rather than surrender. Moreover, if some Confederates took no prisoners, so too did some black regiments.

Black participation in the war was important. The fact that blacks had fought for freedom bolstered black confidence and pride. Military service also carried with it an assumption of American citizenship. Frederick Douglass commented: 'Once let the black man get upon his person the brass letters US, let him get an eagle on his buttons and musket on his shoulder ... and there is no power on earth which can deny that he has earned the right to citizenship in the United States'.

There may have been a tendency recently to exaggerate the impact of black soldiers on the outcome of the war. Some 37,000 black soldiers died in the war. But only 3,000 died in combat: 30,000 died from illness; the fate of 4,000 others is uncertain. Black soldiers fought only at the end. They did not take part in the crucial battles of 1863. But nevertheless there seems little doubt that the influx of black troops had a positive effect on the Union war effort at a critical time when Northern whites were increasingly reluctant to fight. In September 1864 Lincoln wrote:

1 Any different policy in regard to the coloured man [than black recruitment] deprives us of his help and this is more than we can bear ... This is not a question of sentiment or taste, but one of physical force which can be measured and estimated as [can] horse
5 power and Steampower ... Keep it up and you can save the Union. Throw it away and the Union goes with it.

By April 1865 there were nearly as many black soldiers in arms against the Confederacy as there were white soldiers defending it.

6 The Thirteenth Amendment

Lincoln's Emancipation Proclamation was an executive order that would have questionable force once the war ended. In consequence, many Republicans determined to extend the basis of emancipation by passing a constitutional amendment prohibiting slavery. In 1863 a huge petition campaign was waged and some 400,000 signatures were obtained. In April 1864, the Senate passed the constitutional amendment by 38 votes to 6. Democrat opposition in the House prevented the measure from receiving the two-thirds support needed.

In June 1864 Lincoln urged the Republican national convention which met at Baltimore 'to put into the platform as the key stone' a plank endorsing a constitutional amendment to end slavery. The convention did as he asked. Interpreting the Republican election success in November 1864 as a mandate for the anti-slavery amendment, Lincoln redoubled his efforts to secure Congressional approval, applying patronage pressure to several Democrats in the House - to good effect. On 31 January 1865 the House approved (with three votes to spare) the - Thirteenth - Amendment for ratification by the states. The radical Thaddeus Stevens remarked that, 'The greatest measure of the 19th century was passed by corruption, aided and abetted by the purest man in America'. Lincoln was delighted that the amendment was passed. He announced it was 'a King's cure for all the evils. It winds the whole thing up'.

7 The Situation in the South

Most black Americans remained slaves throughout the Civil War. As such, and given that they comprised more than a third of the population of the Confederacy, they made a major contribution to the Confederate war effort. They worked in factories and mines, maintained the railways, helped grow crops, and had an important military role, digging trenches, erecting fortifications and helping behind the lines. Many Southern states passed laws requiring slave owners to furnish their bondsmen for military labour. In 1863 an increasingly desperate Confederate government passed a general impressment law. The utilisation of slave labour undoubtedly enabled the South to fight on longer than would otherwise have been possible.

While most Southerners remained determined to preserve slavery, the war had a major impact on slave-master relations. As the conflict intensified, there were fewer white men left on the farms and plantations to provide supervision of slave labourers. Supervision, therefore, fell to white women, young and old men, and black slave-drivers. Most proved less effective taskmasters than their ante-bellum predecessors. Slaves quickly took advantage of the situation, becoming more insubordinate and working less diligently. (Part of the reason for the drop in their industriousness was the change from cotton to food production - a less intensive form of agricultural labour.) Dislocations caused by the war also undermined authority patterns. Slave owners on the coast or in the path of invading Union armies, desperate to protect their 'property', often sent their slaves to safer areas of the Confederacy. Such uprootings made it difficult physically and psychologically to retain the traditional structure of previously self-contained plantation units.

For many slaves the Civil War was a time of great privation. General shortages of goods resulted in frugal planters cutting back on the food and clothing given to slaves. Male slaves also faced the prospect of impressment. For slaves impressed into front-line labour, the work was not only harder than on the plantation but also more dangerous. Given the possibility of escape through Union lines, slaves at the front were much more closely supervised than on their home farms. Service with the army also cut slaves off from their families. During the war, threatening to send a slave to the front became the disciplinary equivalent of threatening to sell a slave farther South in antebellum days.

Despite Southern fears, there was no slave rebellion in the Civil War. This was not because slaves were content with their lot. They were simply not suicidal. During the war slave patrols, composed of the remaining white men, became more energetic and violent in disciplining recalcitrant slaves. Aware that freedom was coming, most slaves bided their time. Relatively few showed much loyalty to their owners. Whenever a convenient opportunity came to escape, most slaves took it. Many did not wait for the Union army to come to them but instead made their way to Union lines. Camps of 'contrabands' collected around each of the major Federal armies in the South. In 1864, as Sherman's army marched through Georgia, the flow of escaped slaves reached mammoth proportions. In the course of the war an estimated 500,000 slaves fled to join Union armies. This had a devastating effect on the Southern economy.

By 1864 some influential Southerners were arguing in favour of arming slaves to fight for the Confederacy. At first most Southerners opposed the idea. 'Whenever we establish the fact that they are a military race, we destroy our whole theory that they are unfit to be free,' said Governor Brown of Georgia. However, in February 1865 Robert E. Lee, desperately short of men, came out in support of arming and freeing slaves.

Lee's support was enough to tilt the balance and in March 1865 the Confederate Congress finally passed a law providing for the arming of 300,000 slaves. The measure came too late. A few black companies were raised but not in time to see action. Some historians think that had the Confederacy recruited slaves sooner, it might have won the war. However, given that most Southerners had gone to war to preserve their peculiar institution it is easy to understand why little was done to arm the Southern slaves. Whether ex-slaves would have fought loyally for the Confederate cause must remain in doubt.

8 Conclusion

The Confederate states had seceded for primarily one state right - the right to preserve slavery within their borders. This decision proved to be the worst possible one white Southerners could have made in order to preserve slavery. From January 1863 Union soldiers fought for the revolutionary goal of a new Union without slavery. Many - but by no means all - Northern soldiers came to accept this. Most would not have accepted it in 1861. During the war Northern public opinion changed. Abraham Lincoln's policies reflected that change. Lincoln was perhaps not the 'Great Emancipator' of legend. Although he had always considered slavery a moral evil, he moved cautiously on the emancipation issue, his actions based more on pragmatism than on morality. From start to finish, his main aim was to preserve the Union, not free the slave. But by 1862 Lincoln realised that the two issues had become nearly one and the same. By freeing the slaves he could help ensure the preservation of the Union. His Emancipation Proclamation was a vital step forward and a major blow against the Confederacy.

By 1865 many abolitionists were prepared to give credit where credit was due. In February 1865 Garrison (who had castigated Lincoln for being a 'wet rag' in 1862) commended him for having done a 'mighty work for the freedom of millions ... I have the utmost faith in the benevolence of your heart, the purity of your motives and the integrity of your spirit'. The black leader Frederick Douglass commented: 'Viewed from the genuine abolition ground, Mr Lincoln seemed tardy, cold, dull and indifferent; but measuring him by the sentiment of his country, a sentiment he was bound as a statesman to consult, he was swift, zealous, radical and determined'.

Making notes on 'The Destruction of Slavery'

Your notes from this chapter should help you understand the process by which emancipation occurred, the considerations that Abraham Lincoln had to take into account when formulating policy, the impact of the war on African Americans, and the contribution made by African Americans to the outcome of the war. The headings and sub-headings used in the chapter should help you to organise the material.

Answering essay questions on 'The Destruction of Slavery'

It is likely you will use information from this chapter to answer questions on Lincoln's emancipation policy, the process by which slavery was destroyed, and the role of African Americans in the Civil War. Here are two examples:

1   To what extent does Abraham Lincoln deserve the accolade 'The Great Emancipator'?
2   Assess the contribution made by African Americans to Union victory in the Civil War.

Question 1 asks you to focus on Lincoln's role. Be careful that you do not write a narrative essay rather than an analytical one. You will need to consider the pressures upon Lincoln in 1861. Should he be praised or blamed for moving so cautiously? You will have your own views on this.

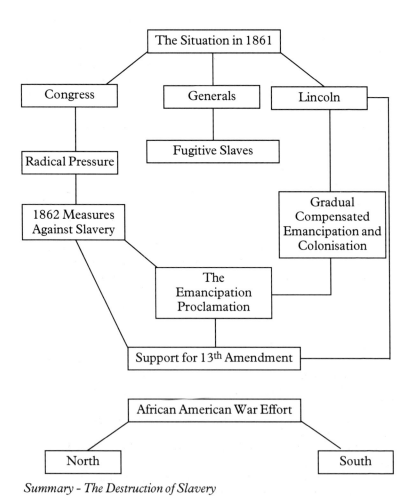

Summary - The Destruction of Slavery

It is something of a moral question. However much historians might try, they cannot avoid the moral dimension to their subject. It would obviously be unfair to judge Lincoln purely by 'politically correct' twentieth-century standards (whatever they are!). Remember that Lincoln, by mid-nineteenth-century American standards, was very much a liberal on the slavery issue. But he did not let his heart rule his head. In my view his policies were determined more by pragmatism than by his conscience but (and this is the important point!) he was right to act as he did. But do not let me persuade you. It is for you to decide. Provided you have evidence to support your view no examiner worth his or her salt will penalise you and most will reward you for a clear (and fair!) answer. Write a conclusion (of about eight sentences) for this question.

Question 2 asks you to assess the African American contribution to Union victory. This question cannot really be answered until you have read Chapters 8 and 9 which look at the process by which the Union won and historians' views about why the Confederacy lost. However, it is certainly possible at this stage to make a list of what contribution blacks made in the war. Make that list - and come back to it after you have read Chapters 8 and 9.

Source-based questions on 'The Destruction of Slavery'

1 Lincoln's views in 1861
Read Lincoln's comments on slavery on pages 105 and 107. Answer the following questions:
a) Explain Lincoln's motives in sending a letter to Virginia in April 1861. (2 marks)
b) Comment on Lincoln's view that, 'I believe I have no lawful right [to interfere with slavery] ... and I have no intention to so do' (3 marks)
c) What exactly had Frémont announced in his proclamation? (2 marks)
d) What does Senator Browning seem to have urged Lincoln to do and what was Lincoln's response? (3 marks)

2 Lincoln's views in September 1862
Read Lincoln's comments to the Chicago ministers on page 110. Answer the following questions:
a) What, in Lincoln's view, was the 'fundamental idea' of the war? (2 marks)
b) On which issues were Lincoln and the Chicago ministers in agreement? (3 marks)
c) What was the main point of difference between Lincoln and the ministers? (3 marks)
d) Why was it unusual that Lincoln was saying what he was saying in this extract in September 1862? (2 marks)

CHAPTER 7

Britain and the Civil War

1 Introduction

Realising from the outset that the Confederacy's best hope of success was if Britain and/or France joined the war on its side, Jefferson Davis tried to secure European recognition and support. In May 1861 Confederate commissioners gained an informal interview with British Foreign Secretary Lord John Russell and argued the legitimacy of the Confederacy's existence and its intention to cultivate mutually profitable relations with Britain. The Russian minister in Washington was quite convinced that, 'England will take advantage of the first opportunity to recognise the seceded States'. In the event, however, neither Britain nor any other foreign power even recognised the Confederacy, never mind intervened on its behalf. Historians debate whether this was the result of good fortune, Northern diplomatic skill, or Southern diplomatic incompetence.

2 Britain's Attitude to the War

Britain, given its great naval, economic, financial and imperial strength (including possession of Canada), was the key European power. Only Britain could mount a serious challenge to the Union. Britain had important historical, political and economic ties with the USA. Nevertheless, prior to the Civil War, relations between the two countries had been soured by mutual resentments that had festered since the American Revolution and been amplified during the War of 1812. Disagreements over fishing and trade agreements, competing interests in Central America and disputes over the Canadian-United States boundaries developed with disturbing regularity. Pre-1861 many British officials held a jaundiced view of Americans and harboured suspicions that the United States was capable of all manner of international mischief.

Prime Minister Lord Palmerston and Foreign Secretary Russell played vital roles in determining British policy. Both knew that there were good reasons for supporting the Confederacy. Britain's immediate and long-term self-interest might well be served by the break-up of the United States - a potential rival to Britain in the none-too-distant future. An independent Confederacy would almost certainly have very stong economic links with Britain, providing Britain with cotton in return for British (rather than Northern) manufactured goods. Cotton was also of immediate concern. Some 20 per cent of British people were dependent on cotton for a living. Given the Union blockade, there seemed a distinct possibility of massive unemployment, possibly leading to the type of disorder which could threaten Britain's social stability. Some feared that, in order to prevent revolution at home, it might be necessary to break the Northern blockade to acquire Southern cotton.

But there were many good reasons for not getting involved in the American conflict. War with the North might easily result in the loss of Canada. It would certainly result in the loss of valuable markets and investments in the North. There was also an awareness that Britain was increasingly dependent on North American grain. The impact of a 'cotton famine' in Britain would be minimal compared to the effects of the 'wheat famine' which might result if Britain waged war against the North.

Palmerston and Russell also knew that British public opinion was far from united. Historians once implied that the upper classes, largely

A British cartoon

because they disliked Yankee manners and values, supported the aristocratic South, while the working classes supported the democratic North. But this view is now recognised as being far too simplistic. Although Northerners (including Lincoln) liked to think that the British working classes were on their side, the reality was that opinion among people of all classes was divided. Evidence suggests that throughout Lancashire (with its vested interest in cotton), there was widespread pro-Southern feeling. Some (including some radicals) sympathised with the Confederacy's aim to win independence and thought the North had no right to force people back into an unpopular Union against their will. There was also a natural sympathy for the under-dog. Given that four slave states remained in the Union, slavery did not seem to be a crucial issue. Indeed, Lincoln's administration insisted for most of 1861 and 1862 that the conflict was not a crusade to abolish slavery. This made it easier for many influential newspapers, like *The Times,* to support the Confederacy.

But a large minority (possibly a majority), aware that slavery lay at the heart of the conflict, supported the North. Radicals like Richard Cobden and John Bright regarded the United States as a role model for Britain. Concerned that the secession of the Confederate states was a blow for democratic progress, they hoped that a Union victory would provide a telling case for a new reform act in Britain which would give more people the vote. Within Palmerston's cabinet, the Duke of Argyll and W.E. Forster were outspokenly pro-Union. Even Confederate sympathisers in Britain were reluctant to get involved in war - a war which most informed opinion believed the Confederacy could win on its own. The Crimean War had indicated the horrors of modern war and the difficulties (and cost) of fighting a war thousands of miles from home. For Palmerston, an exponent of the art of realpolitik, the best solution seemed to be to avoid entanglement, if that was possible.

Palmerston realised it might not be possible. No matter what policy Britain adopted, it was likely that one antagonist or the other would criticise her for taking sides. Seward and Lincoln, for example, were furious that Russell had held 'unofficial' meetings with the Confederate representatives. Palmerston, who distrusted Seward and doubted Lincoln's capacity, was well aware that an 'incident' might easily lead to war. One immediate problem was whether Britain should recognise the Confederacy as a separate and sovereign state, as Confederate agents in Britain urged. Lincoln's administration made it clear that the conflict was a domestic insurrection and not a war. Recognition of the Confederacy, in consequence, was tantamount to a declaration of war against the United States. However, in legal terms the situation was somewhat confused because in April 1861 Lincoln had proclaimed a blockade against the Confederacy. A blockade was usually seen as an instrument of war. (It was absurd to think of a nation blockading its own ports!) Thus it was possible to claim that Lincoln's government had recognised in fact, if not in law, the belligerency of the South. If a state of war existed, Britain could make a reasonable case for at least recognising the Confederacy.

In May 1861 the British government adopted a compromise position. While declaring its neutrality and not recognising the Confederacy as a sovereign state, Britain at least recognised the Confederacy's belligerent status. (France took similar action.) This was more than just words. In British eyes the Confederates were now more than just rebels. Under international law belligerents had the right to contract loans and purchase arms in neutral nations. Britain, therefore, would not go out of its way to prevent trade between British merchants and agents of the Confederacy. Both Lincoln and Seward were appalled by Britain's action. However, the neutrality proclamation forbade British subjects to engage in sympathetic activities on behalf of the Confederacy, prevented the fitting out of warships in British ports, and recognised the Union blockade. (The Treaty of Paris (1856) had declared that a blockade to be legally binding must also be effective: Britain assumed it was!) Having declared itself neutral, the British government made every effort to remain so throughout the contest.

3 Confederate Hopes and Actions

The Confederate government pinned considerable hopes on achieving support from Britain and France. At the very least the Confederacy needed to purchase military supplies, without which it could hardly fight the war. In 1861 most Southerners put their faith in 'King Cotton', believing that Britain and France would be forced to recognise the Confederacy and break the blockade because of their need of 'white gold'. (Of the cotton used in the textile industries of Britain and France 75 per cent came from the Confederate states.) In order to tighten the screw, an unofficial, 'voluntary' - but very effective - cotton embargo was introduced. While the Confederate Congress refused to establish a formal embargo, local 'committees of public safety' in the Southern seaports effectively halted the export of cotton. The *Charleston Mercury* summed up the argument in June 1861: 'the cards are in our hands and we intend to play them out to the bankruptcy of every cotton factory in Great Britain and France or the acknowledgement of our independence'.

Unfortunately for the Confederacy, the embargo ploy failed. European warehouses were full of stocks of cotton purchased in 1859-60, and there was thus no immediate shortage of cotton. Indeed in 1861 the embargo was a blessing in disguise for many textile manufacturers who were forced to put workers on short time, not because of the shortage of cotton, but because the market was saturated with cotton cloth. In consequence, British factory owners did not clamour for intervention. Critics of Confederate policy claim that the cotton embargo backfired. Southerners failed to sell their most valuable commodity at a time when the Northern blockade was at its least effective. (The dearth of cotton for shipment also created the unwanted and false impression that the Northern blockade was effective!) The sale of cotton would have helped the Confederacy purchase more essential supplies in Europe. Moreover, the embargo, an obvious form of economic blackmail, angered Europeans who might otherwise have been sympathetic to the South. 'To intervene on behalf of the South because they have kept cotton from us would be ignominious beyond measure,' said Russell in 1861.

The Confederate ploy, however, might have worked. There was certainly talk at high levels of Britain breaking the Northern blockade. William Gladstone, Chancellor of the Exchequer, favoured British intervention to stop the war and reopen the flow of cotton. In October 1861 Palmerston and Russell agreed that the cotton question might become 'serious' by the end of the year. 'We cannot allow some millions of our people to perish to please the Northern states,' said Palmerston. British and French diplomats discussed the possibility of joint action to lift the blockade. In the event, however, the talks were not followed by action, if only because, on the whole, the British government leaned to the Union - certainly while it held the upper hand on land and sea.

The Confederacy did its best. Agents like James Mason were sent across the Atlantic to argue the Confederate cause and to try to gain access to people in high places. Confederate commissioners established many contacts with British MPs who represented their views in Parliament. The Confederacy, in an attempt to influence British opinion, also set up a newspaper, the *Index,* devoted to presenting the Confederate case. (The paper won respect for its accurate reporting of events.) Cotton diplomacy was successful in obtaining European loans and bonds, guaranteed with cotton. Confederate purchasing agents had spectacular successes purchasing British armaments. Given the British government's firm neutral stance, it is difficult to see what more Confederate diplomats could have done.

4 Union Diplomacy

Northern politicians and diplomats, from Lincoln downwards, are often praised for their dealings with Britain during the Civil War. It has even been claimed that Union victory was won more by Northern diplomats than by Northern soldiers. However, given the fact that the British government and public had no desire for war, this claim should not be pushed too far. Charles Francis Adams, the US minister in London, is usually seen as playing an essential role. His efforts - and the fact that he was personally on good terms with Russell - contributed to frustrating Confederate diplomacy. Praise for Adams's relentless pursuit of Union objectives in Britain is not undeserved. However, the fact that Adams could make use of official channels gave him a massive advantage over the Confederate agents.

William Seward is also often praised for his blunt and at times threatening attitude to Britain. He seemed, according to one contemporary, to be 'an ogre fully resolved to eat all Englishmen raw'. A good example of Seward's tough stance was in May 1861. Learning that Russell had received Confederate commissioners, he prepared a letter so menacing that Lincoln modified some passages and eliminated others. Even in its revised form the dispatch was little less than an ultimatum, suggesting that the United States would break diplomatic relations if Russell persisted in seeing the Southern envoys. The fact that Seward made it abundantly clear that the North would unhesitatingly declare war on any European nation which extended aid or recognition to the Confederacy, may have prevented Britain slipping accidentally into war with the USA. That said, however, Seward's anti-British stance might have been counter productive. Arguably it served only to alienate the British government and helped cause what were unnecessary crises.

Lincoln, who had little time for foreign affairs, usually left policy to Seward. Only when there was a serious crisis did he interfere. His only real claim to fame in diplomatic terms was two-fold: his handling of the Trent affair (see below); and his realisation of the importance of the Emancipation Proclamation on British and European opinion.

5 The Problem of Neutral Rights

The main difficulty between Britain and the Union was the issue of neutral rights at sea. In previous - and subsequent - wars it was Britain which was concerned with problems associated with maintaining a blockade of Continental Europe. This invariably led to problems with American merchant marine. The Civil War was a situation of poacher turned gamekeeper. The British government, aware of the importance of precedents for the future, was reluctant to question the blockade weapon. Nevertheless, crises arose - the most serious being the *Trent* affair. In November 1861 James Mason and John Slidell, Confederate commissioners to Britain and France respectively, left Cuba for Europe in the *Trent* - a British royal mail steamer. Soon after leaving Havana the *Trent* was stopped, in international waters, by Captain Wilkes, commanding the USS ship the *San Jacinto*. Threatening dire action against the *Trent,* Wilkes forcibly removed Mason and Slidell from the British ship. Wilkes action violated international law and created a wave of anger in Britain. 'You may stand for this but damned if I will,' Palmerston told his cabinet.

Although Prince Albert toned down Russell's response, it still bore the appearance of an ultimatum. Britain demanded that Mason and Slidell should be released and the United States must make a public apology for the affair. Uncertain what might happen, the British cabinet set up a War Committee: the British fleet was prepared for action and thousands of British soldiers were sent to Canada. Britain also stopped the export of essential war materials, including salt petre, a prime ingredient of gunpowder, to the Union.

The Trent affair posed a serious dilemma for Lincoln. He was aware that there was a real danger of war if his government did not satisfy Britain. But if he cravenly gave in to Britain, American opinion would be outraged. Wilkes had become something of a national hero in the North, so much so that the House of Representatives had passed a resolution praising his action and voted him a gold medal. Lincoln sensibly played for time allowing heated passions to cool. A compromise was eventually found, for which Lincoln and Seward (who advised that the Union should not risk war against Britain) both deserve some credit. Seward's response to the British demand, a masterpiece of flannel: while not apologising for Wilkes' action, he admitted he had committed an illegal act; and he accepted that Mason and Slidell should be liberated and allowed to sail to Britain.

Even so, relations between the Union and Britain remained strained for much of 1862. Small things could precipitate crises. Palmerston, for example, was outraged by General Butler's May 1862 order in New Orleans that any woman who insulted a Northern soldier 'shall be regarded and held liable to be treated as a woman of the town plying her association'. But Palmerston blew hot and cold. In mid-July he warded off a parliamentary motion for Confederate recognition, even though a majority in the House of Commons favoured such a step.

6 British Mediation?

The closest the Confederacy came to getting British recognition was in August 1862 after its triumph at Second Manassas. Napoleon III's proposal that Britain and France should do all they could to mediate in the conflict was seriously considered by Palmerston and Russell. Both men, motivated more by humanitarian than political or economic concern, hoped to help bring about an end to the war. On 14 September 1862 Palmerston wrote to Russell:

1 The detailed accounts given in the *Observer* to-day of the battles of
  August 29 and 30 between the Confederates and the Federals
  show that the latter got a very complete smashing; and it seems not
  altogether unlikely that still greater disasters await them, and that
5 even Washington or Baltimore may fall into the hands of the
  Confederates. If this should happen, would it not be time for us to
  consider whether in such a state of things England and France
  might not address the contending parties and recommend an
  arrangement upon the basis of separation?

Russell's response (on 17 September) was positive:

1 I agree with you that the time is coming for offering mediation to
the United States Government, with a view to the recognition of
the independence of the Confederates. I agree further that, in case
of failure, we ought ourselves to recognise the Southern States as
5 an independent State. For the purpose of taking so important a
step, I think we must have a meeting of the Cabinet. The 23rd or
30th would suit me for the meeting. We ought then, if we agree on
such a step, to propose it first to France, and then on the part of
England and France, to Russia and other powers, as a measure
10 decided upon by us.

On 23 September Palmerston replied:

1 Your plan of proceedings about the mediation between the
Federals and the Confederates seems to be excellent ... Might it
not be well to ask Russia to join England and France in the offer of
mediation? ... We might be better without her in the mediation,
5 because she would be too favourable to the North; but on the other
hand her participation in the offer might render the North the
more willing to accept it.

Given that mediation meant recognition of the Confederacy, Britain and
France might easily have found themselves at war with the Union. But
the failure of Lee's Maryland invasion convinced Palmerston that it
would not be wise to intervene. Some members of his cabinet still
wanted to take action. In October 1862 Gladstone claimed that
'Jefferson Davis and other leaders have made an army, and are making,
it appears, a navy, and they have made what is more than either, they
have made a nation'. Supported by Gladstone, Russell in mid-October
prepared a memorandum arguing for mediation. But Palmerston and
the rest of his cabinet rejected it. The best hope of European
intervention on the side of the Confederacy had gone. After Lincoln
issued his Emancipation Proclamation, it was highly unlikely that
Britain would risk war against the Union.

The full impact of the cotton shortage finally hit Britain over the
winter of 1862-3 and caused high unemployment in - and widespread
pro-Southern feeling throughout - Lancashire. But, given that the
British economy was generally prospering as a result of the Civil War,
there was limited pressure on the government to take action. During
1863 both the cotton supply and employment began to recover, largely
as a result of increased imports of cotton from India and Egypt.

7 Commerce Raiders

Although denied British recognition, the Confederacy received valuable, if clandestine, assistance from Britain. In spite of Britain's neutrality proclamation, Confederate agents worked effectively to secure British military supplies and equipment. To a great degree the Confederacy's military capacity was enhanced by war materials obtained from Britain in exchange for cotton. In particular, British shipbuilders supplied vessels for a variety of Confederate purposes. The majority were employed in running cargoes through the Union blockade. But the Confederacy was also able to purchase commerce raiders from Britain. In theory the British Foreign Enlistment Act forbad the construction and armament of warships in British territory for a belligerent power. However, Confederate agents got round this by purchasing unarmed ships and then adding the guns and ammunition elsewhere. Palmerston's administration, despite protests from Lincoln's government, essentially shut its eyes to the violation of neutrality by British shipbuilders.

Confederate commerce raiders caused considerable damage to Northern merchant shipping. The *Florida,* for example took 38 prizes between 1863 and 1864. The *Alabama* did even better taking 64 prizes before finally being sunk off Brest. Altogether the North lost some 200 ships to the raiders. While scarcely crippling Northern trade, the raiders were a thorn in the side of the North and something of a humiliation. The raiding activity drove Northern shipping insurance rates to astonishing heights. The consequence was that more and more transAtlantic trade was transferred from costly American to cheaper neutral ships, which were not attacked by the Confederate raiders. So difficult did it become to fund American ships that many had to be sold to foreign buyers. By 1865 over half the American merchant fleet had been effectively lost. The main beneficiary was not the Confederacy but Britain, whose merchant marine toppled America from its once dominant position.

The last serious crisis between the Union and Britain came during the summer of 1863. Lincoln's government was aware that the British shipbuilders Laird Brothers were building two ironclads for the Confederacy. These boats - the so-called Laird rams - would be the strongest ships afloat with the potential to cause massive damage to the North. (The distinguishing feature of the vessels was a heavy iron ram that projected forward about 7 feet from the bow, in theory enabling them to sink an enemy by smashing its hull.) Charles Adams felt so strongly about the issue that he threatened war against Britain if the boats were sold to the Confederacy. The British government, as Adams was aware, had no intention of allowing the 'rams' to be sold and in the end both vessels went into service with the Royal Navy.

The settlement of the Laird rams dispute effectively smoothed

Anglo-Union relations. Although a number of angry letters were exchanged in 1864 as a result of Confederate activity in Canada, this was never more than storm in a teacup. In August 1863 the Confederate Secretary of State Benjamin, convinced that Britain would never grant recognition, ordered James Mason to conclude his mission and withdraw from London.

8 French Policy

From the outset, the French Emperor Napoleon III was keener to get involved in the American Civil War than Britain. He hoped for and expected a Confederate victory. France had similar cotton interests to Britain. Napoleon also had - imperialist - ambitions in Mexico and was aware that he stood a better chance of realising his dream if the United States splintered. But Napoleon was not prepared to take on the Union navy without British support. Palmerston, suspicious of Napoleon's global designs, was not keen to work closely with the French Emperor nor embark on a course of action which might further those designs. Nor could Napoleon count on the French people, most of whom seem to have been apathetic about events in the USA.

Events in Mexico complicated French policy. By 1862 thousands of French soldiers were fighting in Mexico, their avowed purpose being to enforce the collection of Mexican debts. The real purpose, however, was to turn the country into a French colony. In 1864 French troops helped install the Austrian Archduke Maximillian, a French puppet, as Emperor of Mexico. Lincoln's administration was furious at France's action but decided there was little effectively it could do. One war at a time was Lincoln's maxim. Nevertheless Seward made it clear that the United States would not tolerate a French-sponsored Emperor in Mexico.

The Confederate government was prepared to tolerate, even support, French action in Mexico, if this ensured French support. Napoleon, however, determined to avoid a confrontation with the United States, refused to recognise the Confederacy. In 1864 the Confederate government complained that Napoleon had persistently exhibited a friendship for the South and yet with equal persistence, had maintained open and cordial relations with the North. There was little the Confederacy could do about it.

9 Conclusion

One of Palmerston's favourite sayings was: 'They who in quarrels interpose, will often get a bloody nose'. Given his cautious policy, it was always unlikely that Britain would get involved in the Civil War. Britain provided a lead to the rest of Europe, especially France. After the war, it was estimated that British war material for the Confederacy extended the war by as much as two years. But in general Britain's policy of neutrality probably worked to the advantage of the Union. Seward, Lincoln and Adams deserve some credit for their diplomatic skill. But this should not be overrated. Despite Confederate expectations in 1861, it was always unlikely that Britain would get involved. In the circumstances it is hard to see what more the Confederacy could have done to win British recognition. Only if the Confederacy looked like winning would Britain recognise the Confederacy. Yet only if Britain recognised the Confederacy and went to war on her side, was it likely that the Confederacy would achieve success.

Making notes on 'Britain and the Civil War'

Your notes on this chapter should give you an understanding of the international dimension of the Civil War. Arguably, the Confederacy's best hope of victory was to win British support. Confederate leaders were confident that cotton diplomacy would pressure Britain into war. So where did Confederate diplomacy go wrong? Did it go wrong? What could the Confederacy have done that was different? Were the diplomatic odds - like so many other odds - piled too heavily against the Confederacy? How skilful, by contrast, were Union diplomats? Was their success more luck than judgement?

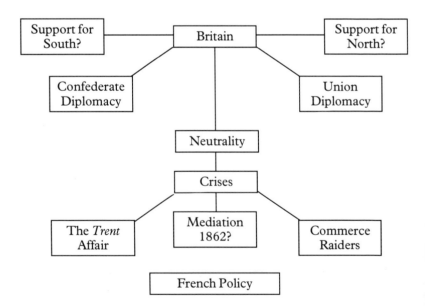

Summary - Britain and the Civil War

Source-based questions on 'Britain and the Civil War'

1 The prospect of British mediation
Read the extracts from the letters written by Palmerston and Lord John Russell on pages 126-7. Answer the following questions:
a) What does the first extract show of the British government's awareness of events in the United States? (2 marks)
b) Comment on the following extract from Palmerston's first letter: 'would it not be the time for us to consider whether … England and France might not address the contending parties and recommend an arrangement upon the basis of separation?' (4 marks)
c) How did Palmerston's proposed course of action differ from that proposed by Russell? (4 marks)

2 British Cartoon
Examine the cartoon on page 121 and answer the following questions:
a) Comment on the title of 'The American Twins' cartoon. (4 marks)
b) Which side - North or South - does 'The American Twins' cartoonist support? Explain your answer. (6 marks)

CHAPTER 8

The End of the War

1 'Simultaneous Movement All Along the Line'

In March 1864 Lincoln, in preparation for the new campaigning season, again reorganised his army command structure. U.S. Grant was now named General-in-Chief of all the Union armies. Sherman took Grant's place in the West. Meade continued in control of the Army of the Potomac while Halleck became Chief of Staff. Grant immediately came east to supervise the effort to destroy Lee. Although Lincoln had faith in his new General-in-Chief, many Army of the Potomac veterans remained sceptical. Despite his victories in the West, Grant had still to fight Lee.

Grant's proposed strategy was simple. Determined to make use of the Union's greater manpower, he called for a 'simultaneous movement all along the line'. The 115,000-strong Army of the Potomac would attack Lee. 'Lee's army will be your objective point,' Grant told Meade. 'Wherever Lee goes, there you will go also'. Sherman's Western army would capture Atlanta and then 'get into the interior of the enemy's country ... inflicting all the damage you can'. The 30,000 men in Louisiana under Nathaniel Banks were to capture Mobile and then head northwards. General Butler, who commanded a 30,000-strong Union army at Yorktown, was to approach Richmond up the York-James peninsula. Finally Franz Sigel's 26,000 men were to march up the Shenandoah Valley. Lincoln approved of this strategy: it was the strategy he had advocated from the start.

The Confederacy by 1864 had to scrape the bottom of its manpower barrel. Men between the ages of 17 and 50 were now liable for conscription. Even so, Confederate forces were less than half those of the North. Southern soldiers were short of everything - especially food. However, the morale of the Army of North Virginia remained high and General Joe Johnston, reappointed to command the Army of Tennessee, had done a good job in improving morale in the West after the disasters at Chattanooga. Although they would be outnumbered in the coming campaigns, at least most Confederate soldiers were veterans. Many Union veterans, on the other hand, were due to go home in 1864 when their three-year enlistment period ended. This would seriously weaken the Federal army. Rather than require the veterans to re-enlist, the Union relied on persuasion and inducement offering a 30-days-furlough and a $400 bounty. If 75 per cent of men in a regiment re-enlisted, the regiment retained its identity. Some 136,000 Federal veterans, scenting victory, re-enlisted; 100,000 decided not to do so.

2 Grant's Plan Unfolds

Grant's grand plan did not go entirely as expected in the summer of 1864. Banks got totally bogged down in the Red River area and never reached Mobile. Butler failed to exert pressure on Richmond. Union forces in the Shenandoah Valley were similarly ineffective. Indeed in July 1864 a 10,000 Confederate force pushed up the Shenandoah Valley and reached the suburbs of Washington, forcing Grant to send reinforcements to defend the Northern capital.

The Army of the Potomac had mixed success. With a two-to-one superiority in manpower, Grant was determined to take the initiative, hoping to manoeuvre Lee into an open-field combat. Lee's strategy was straightforward: to keep Grant from Richmond; force him to attack fortified positions; and make the cost of trying to defeat the Confederacy so high that Northerners would refuse to pay the price and vote out Lincoln in the November 1864 presidential election. In May 1864 Grant crossed the Rapidan river, threatening to slip round Lee's right flank. The bloodiest six weeks of the war now began. On 5-6 May Union and Confederate forces met again in the same Wilderness that had foiled

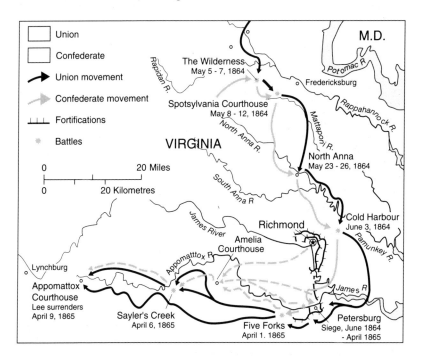

Virginia Campaign 1864-1865

Hooker one year earlier. The Federal army suffered 18,000 casualties in confused, ferocious fighting - twice the losses sustained by Lee. But Grant (unlike Hooker in 1863) had no intention of retreating. Instead he edged southwards, trying to get between Lee and Richmond. For the next month the opposing armies were never out of contact and were fighting or digging virtually every day and night. Grant's probings were foiled by Lee's skilful defence. On 3 June at Cold Harbour Grant lost 7,000 men in just over one hour: Lee lost 1,500. (This was the only action which Grant later said he regretted.) In the first 30 days of his offensive, Grant lost 50,000 men - twice as many as Lee. Northern Democrats denounced him as 'Butcher' Grant. But the slogging match had just as great an impact on the Army of Northern Virginia. By June Lee was desperately short of men and material and many of his most trusted commanders were dead or seriously wounded.

Grant's perseverance paid off. In June Union forces crossed the James river, threatening Richmond from the south and almost capturing Petersburg, a crucial railway junction. Sheer luck and inspired resistance from a small force led by Beauregard saved the day for the Confederacy. Lee, aware that the loss of Petersburg would result in the loss of Richmond, had little option but to defend the town. Both sides dug trenches and the siege of Petersburg began. On 30 July the Federal army tried to blast a way through the Confederate defences, exploding tons of gunpowder below the Confederate lines. But in the fighting which followed, Union forces got bogged down in the crater created by the explosion and suffered 4,500 casualties. The Confederates hung on.

Although Grant had not yet defeated Lee, he had at least forced him on to the defensive and ensured he was no longer able to fight the type of war at which he excelled - a war of manoeuvre. Both Grant and Lee knew that a war of attrition favoured the Union. In spite of the huge casualties sustained in May and June, Grant ended the 1864 Virginia campaign with more men than when he started. Lee had fewer men and his army was to be further reduced by sickness, desertion and constant Union probing. Grant also kept threatening Lee's flank so he had to lengthen Confederate earthworks, thus reducing the number of men who held each yard of ground.

In the autumn of 1864 the Confederacy also suffered serious setbacks in the Shenandoah Valley. Sheridan, the new Union commander, chased the Confederates up the Valley, deliberately destroyed everything en route and winning crucial battles at Winchester and at Cedar Creek. The Shenandoah Valley was now firmly under Union control.

3 The Atlanta Campaign

In May 1864 Sherman, with 100,000 men, left Chattanooga and headed towards Atlanta, state capital of Georgia and an important industrial and communications centre. His Confederate opponent, General Johnston commanded some 70,000 men. Although Johnston had done a creditable job restoring the Army of Tennessee's morale, he had also spent much of 1863-4 bickering with the Confederate government. Johnston and Davis (who hated each other) were unable to reach any agreement about what strategy to adopt and were soon working at cross purposes. Rather than go on the offensive - as Davis wanted - Johnston retreated into Georgia, taking up strong positions and hoping Sherman would launch costly frontal offensives. Instead Sherman repeatedly turned Johnston's flank, forcing the Confederates back to the next prepared position. Sherman did try one frontal attack at Kenesaw Mountain in June but this was a disaster. Thereafter he returned to his flanking manoeuvres. Johnston failed to use his cavalry to cut the frail Federal supply line and seemed impervious to the rising discontent over his continuous retreat and consequent surrender of valuable territory. By July Union forces had reached the outskirts of Atlanta. Davis felt - with good reason - that he had no alternative but to remove Johnston. He replaced him with 33-year-old John Bell Hood.

Hood, who had lost an arm at Gettysburg and a leg at Chickamauga, was a brave fighter but had little skill as a commander. 'All lion, none of the fox,' was Lee's view, a view that Hood was now to confirm. Rather than simply defend Atlanta, Hood proceeded to attack well-entrenched Union lines. Each attack was a disaster. Confederate casualties amounted to 20,000 men - far more than Union losses. Having lost one-third of his army, Hood had little alternative but to fall back into Atlanta and the town was besieged. At the end of August, Sherman threatened Hood's railway supply line and the Confederate commander had no option but to abandon Atlanta. Union forces moved into the town on 3 September. The capture of Atlanta was an important boost to Northern morale.

4 The 1864 Election

By 1864 it was clear that the Confederacy's main - indeed last - hope was that Lincoln would be defeated in the presidential election. This hope was a realistic one. In the summer of 1864, with the war going badly, Lincoln was despondent: 'I am going to be beaten and unless some great change takes place, badly beaten,' he wrote in August 1864. The Democrat party hoped to capitalise on Northern war weariness and Lincoln's unpopularity. Most Democrats wanted to preserve the Union but many believed that the time had come to negotiate peace with the Confederacy. In August 1864 the Democrat convention met in Chicago. The party's platform called for a negotiated peace, condemned Lincoln's arbitrary measures, and pledged to preserve states' rights. General McClellan was nominated as Democrat presidential candidate. McClellan, however, would not agree to the peace platform which

THE BEGINNING.

ELECTION OF M'CLELLAN!

PENDLETON, VALLANDIGHAM,
Vice-President.　　　　Secretary of War.

ARMISTICE!

FALL OF WAGES!

NO MARKET FOR PRODUCE!

Pennsylvania a Border State!

INVASION! CIVIL WAR! ANARCHY!

DESPOTISM!!

THE END.

An 1864 Pennsylvania Election Poster

ABRAHAM

AFRICANUS I.

His Secret Life,

AS REVEALED UNDER THE

MESMERIC INFLUENCE.

Mysteries of the White House.

J. F. FEEKS, PUBLISHER,
No. 26 ANN STREET, N. Y.

The front of an 1864 satirical pamphlet

meant that the Democrats were in something of a muddle. In the weeks that followed, their strongest card was accusing Lincoln of being a 'negro-lover' and plotting 'miscegenation' - the blending of the white and black races.

It had been far from certain that Lincoln would win the Republican nomination. In early 1864 many Republicans would like to have nominated General Grant but he made it clear he would not stand. Secretary of the Treasury Chase had presidential ambitions but politically was no match for Lincoln and failed to mount a serious challenge. In the end the most serious threat came from John Frémont - the 1856 Republican candidate. Creating his own political party (the Radical Democrats), it seemed he might split the Republican vote, thus ensuring a Democrat victory. Lincoln, however, had the support of the Republican party as a whole. That party now went under the name of the National Union or Union League. The hope was that the change of name might encourage 'War' Democrats to support Lincoln. Throughout 1864 Republican state committees, legislatures and Union Leagues passed resolutions endorsing Lincoln. It was thus no surprise when he was renominated (on the first ballot) at the Republican/Union League convention at Baltimore in June 1864. The only real contest was generated by the vice presidential nomination. After some obscure backstage manoeuvrings, Andrew Johnson of Tennessee was chosen as Lincoln's running mate. The fact that Johnson was both a Southerner and a War Democrat seemed to add strength to the Republican/Union ticket. The Republican platform endorsed unremitting war to force the unconditional surrender of the Confederacy and called for the 'utter and complete extirpation of slavery' by means of a constitutional amendment. Lincoln's problems were not quite over. In August wide cracks appeared between Lincoln and his party over reconstruction policy. But with the election only a few weeks away, most Republicans remained loyal to Lincoln. (See the accompanying Access book, *Reconstruction and the Results of the American Civil War* for more details on reconstruction.)

In September 1864 the war turned in Lincoln's favour. Atlanta fell; Sheridan was successful in the Shenandoah; and there was a sharp drop in Grant's casualty rate. Frémont now withdrew from the race (urging support for Lincoln) and the election became a straight contest between Lincoln and McClellan. Lincoln, adhering to the traditional role of a presidential candidate, avoided public pronouncements and let others do the 'dirty' political work. Republicans/Unionists, wrapping themselves in the flag, ridiculed McClellan's military record and did their best to depict the Democrats as, at best, unpatriotic defeatists and, at worst, traitors.

In November Lincoln won 2,213,645 popular votes (55 per cent of the total) and 212 electoral college votes to McClellan's 1,802,237 votes (45 per cent) and 21 electoral college votes. The Republicans also succeeded in increasing their (already large) majority in both houses of Congress. The similarity between the Republican/Union vote of 1864 and the Republican vote of 1860 in the Northern states was remarkable. Native-born, Protestant Americans - especially in New England and the Upper North - remained loyal to Lincoln. Particularly remarkable was the backing Lincoln received from Union soldiers. Most states enacted provision for soldiers to vote in the field. Those states which blocked this measure failed to stop the soldiers from voting. The War Department, recognising the overwhelming Republican sympathy of the soldiers, allowed whole regiments to return home to vote. It seems that Lincoln received 78 per cent of the soldier vote - a great achievement considering that some 40 per cent of the soldiers were probably Democrats when they joined the army.

The election had really been a referendum on whether the North should continue fighting. Lincoln's success was very much the death-knell of the Confederacy.

5 Georgia and Tennessee

In the autumn of 1864 Sherman divided his army. Leaving General Thomas to watch Hood and to defend Tennessee, Sherman set off from Atlanta in mid-November with 62,000 men on a march through Georgia to Savannah on the coast. Cutting adrift from supply lines, Sherman's aim was to demoralise the South, destroying both its capacity and its will to fight. Convinced his men could live off the land and aware that the Confederacy was not in a position to mount effective opposition, he was supremely confident. In a letter to Confederate officials in Atlanta in September 1864 he made his intentions clear:

1 You cannot qualify war in harsher terms than I will. War is cruelty, and you cannot refine it: and those who brought war into our country deserve all the curses and maledictions a people can pour out ... Once admit the Union, once more acknowledge the
5 authority of the national Government, and instead of devoting your houses and streets and roads to the dread uses of war, I and this army become at once your protectors and supporters, shielding you from danger ...
   You might as well appeal against the thunder-storm as against
10 these terrible hardships of war. They are inevitable, and the only way the people of Atlanta can hope once more to live in peace and quiet at home, is to stop the war, which can only be done by admitting that it began in error and is perpetuated in pride.
   We don't want your Negroes, or your horses, or your houses, or
15 your lands, or any thing you have, but we do want and will have a just obedience to the laws of the United States. That we will have,

and if it involves the destruction of your improvements, we cannot help it.

Sherman's march - intended to make Georgia 'howl' - went much to plan. His army marched in two columns, throwing out foragers ('bummers') in all directions to supply the troops. Leaving a swathe of destruction some 60 miles wide, Sherman's army finally reached and captured Savannah in mid-December. The march to Savannah cost Sherman around 2,200 casualties: it had inflicted some $100 million damage on Georgia, crippled much of the state's railway network, and given a lie to the Confederate government's promise of protection for its people. Sherman's intention was now to march north through the Carolinas to join up with Grant at Petersburg.

Instead of trying to stop Sherman, Hood decided to launch an attack on Tennessee. His scheme - to defeat Thomas's forces, reconquer Kentucky and then advance to help Lee - came to nothing. On 30 November Hood ordered a suicidal assault on Union forces at Franklin. Confederate losses were three times those of the North. The Union army now pulled back to Nashville which Hood 'besieged' for two severely cold weeks. Given that Hood had 23,000 men and Thomas some 50,000, it was hard to know who was besieging who! Despite pressure from Lincoln, Thomas (one of the Union's unsung heroes) delayed his counter attack until he was fully prepared. When he finally struck on 15-16 December he succeeded in winning the most complete victory of the war. The battle of Nashville effectively destroyed Hood's Army of Tennessee. A few detachments made their way eastward to join other forces still fighting. But other survivors simply went home. In January 1865 Hood resigned what was left of his command.

On 26 December 1864 Lincoln wrote the following letter to

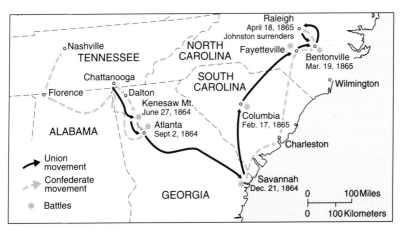

Sherman's march through the South 1864-65

Sherman:

1 Many, many thanks for your Christmas gift - the capture of Savannah. When you were about leaving Atlanta for the Atlantic coast, I was anxious, if not fearful; but feeling that you were the better judge, and remembering that 'nothing risked, nothing
5 gained' I did not interfere. Now, the undertaking being a success, the honour is all yours; for I believe none of us went farther than to acquiesce. And taking the work of Gen. Thomas into the count, as it should be taken, it is indeed a great success. Not only does it afford the obvious and immediate military advantage; but, in
10 showing to the world that your army could be divided, putting the stronger part to an important new service, and yet leaving enough to vanquish the old opposing force of the whole - Hood's army - it brings those who sat in darkness, to see a great light. But what next? I suppose it will be safer if I leave Gen. Grant and yourself to
15 decide. Please make my grateful acknowledgments to your whole army, officers and men.

6 The End of the Confederacy

In his December 1864 address to Congress, Lincoln spoke confidently of victory. Union resources, he said, were unexhausted and inexhaustible: its military and naval forces were larger than ever; its population was growing and its economy was prospering. The Confederacy's situation, on the other hand, was desperate. On paper the Confederacy still had 400,000 men in arms but the reality was very different. Its Western armies were in tatters and Lee's once proud Army of Northern Virginia suffered from mass desertions over the winter as troops received despairing letters from home.

Davis clutched at straws. In December 1864 he sent word by special envoy to Britain and France that he was prepared to emancipate all the Southern slaves in exchange for recognition. But this offer had no effect. In early February the Confederate Vice President Stephens (with Davis's approval) met Lincoln to see if it was possible to arrange peace. The talks were brief and unproductive. Lincoln, confident of victory, was not prepared to compromise on either slavery or disunion and the Confederate government was still not prepared to surrender. Lee, now given overall command of all that was left of the Confederate armies, asked for regiments of slaves to be raised to fight for the Southern cause in return for their freedom. In March, the Confederate Congress finally approved a measure it had previously opposed.

This measure came too late to have any impact on the war. The Confederacy was falling apart. In January 1865 Wilmington, the last major Confederate port, was effectively closed with the Union capture of Fort Fisher. In February Sherman, undeterred by rain, swamp and sporadic resistance, began his march north towards Richmond. South Carolina, blamed by most Northerners as the cause of the war, suffered worse deprivation than Georgia. Confused, frustrated, frightened and angered, the morale of Southerners plummetted. Lee gave Joe Johnston the thankless task of trying to resist Sherman's remorseless march. On 19 March Johnston attacked the head of Sherman's army at Bentonville. The Confederates had some initial success but then were forced to pull back, totally outnumbered. By April Sherman neared Richmond.

Grant did not really need Sherman's army. By March 1865 Confederate trench lines extended 35 miles and Lee had only 35,000 half-starved troops to man them. Grant had 125,000 men, not counting Sheridan approaching from the north and Sherman approaching from the south. At the end of March Lee ordered a desperate assault on Fort Stedman. It failed. On 1 April Union General Sheridan won a decisive victory at Five Forks. The following day Grant ordered a full-scale assault and the Union army broke through Lee's overstretched lines. Lee had no option but to abandon both Petersburg and Richmond. Davis fled. On 3 April Lincoln visited Richmond. Moving about unguarded through the former capital of the Confederacy, he was mobbed by ex-slaves who greeted him as a messiah.

Lee headed westwards, hoping to find supplies for his troops and to join up with Johnston's forces. Instead he found himself surrounded by Union forces. On 6 April, trying to break out of the trap, Lee fought his last battle at Sayler's Creek. He achieved nothing, except the loss of a further 8,000 men - one-third of his army. By 9 April, Lee realised, 'There is nothing left for me to do but to go and see General Grant and I would rather die a thousand deaths'. Lee and Grant met in Wilmer McKlean's parlour at Appomattox Court House. Lee surrendered and Grant was magnanimous in victory, allowing the Confederate army generous terms: troops could keep their side arms, personal possessions and horses; and Grant gave the famished Confederates Northern army rations. Lee, meeting his troops for the last time, said, 'Boys I have done the best I could for you. Go home now, and if you make as good citizens as you have soldiers, you will do well, and I shall always be proud of you'.

Lee's surrender at Appomattox was the effective end of the war. Davis, fleeing southwards, exhorted the Confederacy to fight on and spoke of a new phase of the struggle. But most Southerners heeded Lee's advice and showed no interest in a guerilla war. They had suffered enough. In mid-April Johnston surrendered to Sherman. Davis was finally captured on 10 May. The last skirmish, fought in Texas on 13 May, was ironically a Confederate victory! A handful of rebel partisans, scattered in remote regions, fought on for few more weeks. A Confederate ship, the *Shenandoah*, continued 'fighting' through June, seizing and burning Northern whaling ships, before surrendering in

Liverpool in November 1865.

Abraham Lincoln did not live to deal with the problems left by the Civil War. He was assassinated by the actor - and Confederate sympathiser - John Wilkes Booth on 14 April 1865.

Making notes on *'The End of the War'*

The South's best hope of victory from the start had been to inflict so many casualties on Union forces that most Northerners would come to believe that the war was not worth fighting. In the summer of 1864 the Confederacy seemed near to achieving its aim. But military events then turned against the South and Lincoln's re-election in November 1864 was proof that most Northerners were still committed to winning the war. Your notes should provide you with an outline of the main military and political events pre- and post-November 1864 which led to Union victory in 1865.

Source-based questions on *'The End of the War'*

1 Sherman and Georgia
Read the extract from Sherman's letter to the civilian authorities in Atlanta on pages 138-9 and Lincoln's letter to Sherman on page 140. Answer the following questions:
a)   What (essentially) was Sherman's theory of war? (3 marks)

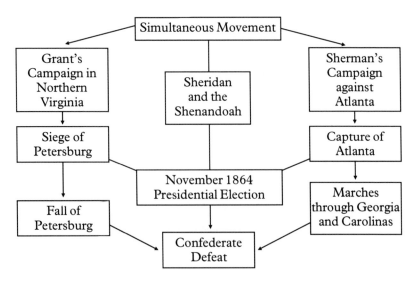

Summary - The End of the War

b) Does this source indicate that Sherman was sympathetic or hostile to the South? (4 marks)
c) Why was Lincoln 'anxious, if not fearful' of Sherman's march to the sea? (4 marks)
d) Why did Lincoln regard Sherman's strategy as a 'great success'? (4 marks)
e) What does Lincoln's letter indicate of his leadership style? (5 marks)

2 The 1864 Election
Examine the election poster and pamphlet on page 136. Answer the following questions:
a) What are the two anti-Lincoln points which the cover of the 'Abraham Africanus 1' pamphlet is trying to make? (2 marks)
b) Explain the main points made in the Pennsylvania broadsheet. (5 marks)
c) What points might a Democrat broadsheet have made? (4 marks)
d) What might have been the main points made by the front cover of an anti-McClellan pamphlet? (4 marks)

CHAPTER 9

Conclusion: The Historiographical Debates

1 Introduction

Efforts to explain Northern victory and Southern defeat have generated a great deal of historical controversy. The debate began almost as soon as the war ended and still continues. James McPherson has stressed that it is dangerous to generalise about the cause of Northern victory/ Confederate defeat. At many stages of the war, events on the battlefield might have gone differently and if they had, the course of the war might have been quite different. Only by looking at each military campaign, each battle, each decision during the war, says McPherson, is it possible to fully understand the war's outcome. Of course, he is right. But nevertheless, historians do and must generalise. Most would accept that there were many causes for Southern defeat/Northern victory. But many would tend to emphasise one or two causes at the expense of others. Some focus mainly or entirely on the Confederacy and usually ask 'Why did the Confederacy lose?' Others, concentrating on the North, ask 'Why did the Union win?'

2 'Big Battalions'

One of the earliest and most durable explanations of Confederate defeat was advanced by Robert E. Lee in his farewell address to his soldiers at Appomattox on April 10, 1865: 'After four years' arduous service, marked by unsurpassed courage and fortitude, the Army of Northern Virginia has been compelled to yield to overwhelming numbers and resources.'

According to Lee, the Confederacy lost the war not because it fought badly or because its soldiers lacked courage, but simply because the enemy had more men and guns. This thesis has had many supporters the twentieth century. The historian Richard Current, reviewing the statistics of Northern strength - two and a half times the South's population, three times its railway capacity, nine times its industrial production, overwhelming naval supremacy - concluded that 'surely in view of the disparity of resources, it would have taken a miracle ... to enable the South to win. As usual, God was on the side of the heaviest battalions'. More recently Shelby Foote declared: 'the North fought that war with one hand behind its back.' If necessary, 'the North simply would have brought that other arm from behind its back. I don't think the South ever had a chance to win that war'.

Yet in 1861 most Southerners and most Europeans thought that Confederate resources were more than sufficient to win the war. Many historians continue to insist that the Confederacy could have triumphed. History offers many examples of a society winning a war against greater odds than the Confederacy faced. The outstanding example in the minds of everyone in 1861 was the United States in its War of Independence against Britain. Superior strategy, leadership and morale can be more important than superior numbers and resources. Many historians, therefore, have rejected the 'big battalions' thesis as a sufficient explanation for Confederate defeat.

3 Divisions within the Confederacy

Some historians have explained Confederate defeat by focusing on divisions within the South. There are several variations on this theme. In 1925 Frank Owsley claimed that support for the notion of state rights fatally crippled the efforts of Davis's government to wage war. Individual states put their own interests before those of the Confederacy. Owsley particularly singled out Governors Brown of Georgia and Vance of North Carolina as guilty of obstructive policies. On the tombstone of the Confederacy, thought Owsley, should be written the epitaph, 'Died of State Rights'. But recent scholarship has shown that the negative effects of state rights' sentiment have been much exaggerated. Governors Brown and Vance did indeed feud with the Davis administration. But the scale of their obstructionism was relatively limited. In reality, Brown and Vance, like the rest of the Southern governors, worked hard to assist the Confederate cause - raising and equipping regiments, organising war production, building coastal defences and so on. Rather than hindering the efforts of the Richmond government, the activities of states augmented them.

A variant of the state rights' thesis focuses on the resistance by many Southerners to such war measures as conscription, direct taxes and martial law. Opponents denounced these 'despotic' measures on grounds of civil liberty, or state rights, or democratic individualism, or all three combined. According to David Donald, the carping criticism of the opposition sapped the people's will, crippled the army's ability to fill its ranks, obtain supplies, and stem desertions, and so weakened the Confederate's war effort that the inscription on the Confederacy's tombstone should be altered to: 'Died of Democracy'. This claim is not particularly convincing. During the war Davis's government enforced the draft, suppressed dissent and suspended civil liberties as thoroughly as did Lincoln's government.

Recent scholarship has focused on three groups in the South that were (or became) alienated from the Confederate war effort: planters, non-slaveholding whites and slaves.

The large plantation owners, it is claimed, discovered that life under the Confederacy was very different from their expectations. Rather than the limited central government they expected, Davis created a strong central government whose bureaucracy was larger in proportion to the Confederate population than the Union bureaucracy. Certainly some Confederate policies (e.g. impressment of slaves) provoked harsh attacks from planters who were well represented in the political arena. However, the view that planter criticism impeded the process of building support for the new nation is not convincing. Most planters remained loyal to the Confederacy from first to last.

Two-thirds of the Confederacy's white population were non-slaveholders. Some opposed secession in 1861. Others became alienated as a result of ruinous inflation, food shortages, high taxes, and a growing suspicion that they were risking their lives and property simply to defend slavery. Clauses in the 1862 Conscription Law that allowed a drafted man to buy a substitute and exempted from the draft one white man on every plantation with 20 or more slaves gave rise to a bitter cry that it was 'a rich man's war and a poor man's fight'. A conviction of class discrimination may have led to a decline in support for the war effort. However, it is easy to exaggerate the extent of non-slaveholders' alienation. McPherson found little evidence of class division in the letters of Confederate soldiers. Many non-slaveholding Southerners were ready to fight and die for the Confederate cause.

Slaves made up 40 per cent of the Southern population and were essential to the Confederate war effort. But while slavery was a source of strength to the Confederacy, it was also a source of weakness. Most slaves were instinctively Unionist. Tens of thousands voted with their feet by escaping to Federal lines, where the North converted first their labour power and eventually their military manpower into a Union asset. This leakage of labour from the Confederacy and the unrest of slaves who remained behind, damaged the Southern economy. However, it was never likely that the Confederacy would persuade the slaves that the creation of a nation based on the continued existence of slavery was desirable. In the circumstances the Confederacy was fortunate that it did not have to face a great slave revolt in its rear.

It is worth remembering that large numbers of Northerners were bitterly opposed to Lincoln's administration. About one-third of the border-state whites actively supported the Confederacy and many of the remainder were at best lukewarm Unionists. Guerilla warfare behind Union lines occurred in these regions on a far larger scale than in Unionist areas behind Confederate lines. If the South had its class conflict over the theme of 'rich man's war: poor man's fight', so did the North. If the Confederacy had its bread riots, the Union had its draft riots. If many soldiers deserted from the Confederate armies, a similarly large percentage deserted from Union armies. If the South had its slaves who wanted Yankee victory, the North had its Democrats and border-state whites who strongly opposed many of Lincoln's measures. Divisions within the Confederacy, therefore, do not, in themselves, provide a sufficient explanation for Confederate defeat.

4 Lack of Will

A major explanation for Confederate defeat holds that the Confederacy could have won if the Southern people had possessed the will to make the sacrifices necessary for victory. The historian E. Merton Coulter declared that the Confederacy lost because its 'people did not will hard enough and long enough to win'.

The first - and main - lack-of-will argument is that the Confederacy, given its short existence, did not generate a strong sense of nationalism and Southerners, therefore, did not have as firm a conviction as Northerners of fighting for a country. Southerners, loyal Americans before they became Confederates, had much in common with Northerners. Thus, when the going got tough, it is claimed, Southerners found it tough to keep going. If the nationalist spirit had been strong enough, the Confederacy would have continued a savage guerilla struggle against Union forces after April 1865.

The lack of nationalism argument, however, is not convincing. Ante-bellum Southerners did have a sense of distinctiveness. What set them apart from the rest of the nation - and the rest of the world - was slavery. Slavery was the cornerstone of the Confederacy's national identity and pride. It was the main reason for secession and the main reason why Southerners fought. The strength of patriotic feeling in 1861 produced 500,000 volunteers for military service. Confederate politicians, clergymen and newspaper editors all did their utmost to create a sense of nationalism. Memories of 1776 - when earlier Americans had succeeded in creating a new nation - were invoked. By claiming American nationalism as their own, Southerners had at once an identity and a history. The war strengthened Southern nationalism. It gave Southerners a new set of heroes. It also created a unifying hatred of the enemy. Hostile images of the Yankee, long current in Southern culture, were magnified. Hatred and a desire for revenge seem to have been consuming passions for many Southern soldiers. But enmity was not the only reason why Southerners fought. McPherson found considerable evidence of simple but very strong patriotism in the letters of Confederate soldiers. Many believed they were fighting for liberty and constitutional rights, principles for which they were ready to die. (In fact, 29 per cent of McPherson's letter sample did die!)

Far from being a weakness, the spirit of nationalism explains why most Southerners fought as long and as hard as they did. It is worth remembering that Southerners persisted through far greater hardship than most Northerners experienced. Northerners almost threw in the towel in the summer of 1864 when they suffered casualty rates that Southerners had endured for more than two years. It is thus possible to claim that Southern nationalism was stronger than its Union counterpart. Certainly the Confederacy endured a great deal in its fight for independence, including a death toll far greater that France's in the

Franco-Prussian War (1870-1). Nobody suggests that the French in 1870 did not have a strong sense of national identity. Their nation was simply defeated by the more powerful Prussians. Nations routinely make war against one another and lose. Nationalism is not a magic shield ensuring invulnerability to those who possess it.

Thus it seems hard to accept the notion that lack of will stemming from weak nationalism was the main cause of Confederate defeat. Nor should it be forgotten that even if the Confederacy was new, many Southerners were tremendously loyal to their individual states which - in many cases - had been long established. Many, like Robert E. Lee in 1861, considered their state to be their 'country'. Like Lee they went with their country and fought for it to the end.

A second lack-of-will interpretation is the notion that many Southern whites felt moral qualms about slavery, which undermined their will to fight a war to preserve it. Kenneth Stampp has argued that many Southerners might actually have 'subconsciously' welcomed defeat. It is hard to believe, however, that moral qualms about slavery brought about Confederate defeat. The vast majority of white Southerners saw it as a positive good. Most remained committed to it. It was one of the chief reasons why they fought and died for four terrible years.

A third lack-of-will interpretation focuses on religion. As the war went on and the South suffered so much death and destruction, some Southerners began to wonder if God was really on their side after all. Several historians think these religious doubts may have helped corrode Confederate morale. However, this viewpoint, ignores the fact thaat most Southern Church leaders had no doubts about the justice of the Southern cause. Over the winter of 1863-4 a great religious revival movement swept through the Confederate army. Rather than explaining Confederate defeat, religion played a vital role in actually sustaining Southern will.

The final lack-of-will argument concentrates on the economic and financial situation. By 1862, as a result of the Northern blockade, there was a shortage of almost everything in the Southern states. The South's inability to maintain its transport system worsened the economic situation. The effects of runaway inflation, brought about by shortages and the issue of huge quantities of paper money, were devastating. Most families were also victimised by impressment or suffered from shortage of labour caused by volunteering and conscription. Severe hardship on the home front led to a relentless growth of defeatism which was conveyed by uncensored letters to Confederate soldiers.

However, there is a significant difference between loss and lack of will. A people whose armies are beaten, railways wrecked, factories and cities burned, countryside occupied and crops laid waste, quite naturally lose their will to continue fighting because they have lost the means to do so. That is what happened to the Confederacy. It was Union military success which created war weariness and destroyed morale. By 1865 the

Confederacy had lost its will for sacrifice. But primarily it was military defeat which caused loss of will, not lack of will which caused military defeat.

Historians have tended to examine why Southern will collapsed rather than ask the (at least equally) important question: why did Northern will hold and prevail. It is often said that the Confederacy had no chance in a war of attrition. In fact a war of attrition was the best - perhaps the only - chance the South had. To win the Confederacy had to wear down Northern will: a long, bloody war was the best way to do this. The war was long and bloody but Northern will endured. Why was this? Strong leadership at every level, from Lincoln downwards, obviously had some effect. The fact that the Northern economy was able to produce both 'guns' and 'butter' helped civilian morale. For many families in the North life during the war went on much the same as usual. Northern losses (relatively) were less than those sustained by Southerners. The North was never seriously invaded and, despite higher taxes, many Northerners experienced increased prosperity during the war. But ultimately Northern will, like Southern will, seems to have been crucially affected by the outcome of campaigns and battles. The morale of Northern soldiers was particularly crucial to Northern victory. In 1861 the Union, like the Confederacy, had no difficulty raising troops. Hundreds of thousands of men, proclaiming love of Union, liberty and democracy, rushed to enlist. McPherson's study of soldiers' letters suggests that Northern soldiers were aware of the issues at stake and passionately concerned about them. For many the war, for all its horrors, remained a crusade. In the 1864 presidential elections some 80 per cent of Northern soldiers voted for Lincoln, proof that soldier morale still held strong. Federal victories from mid-1863 onwards undoubtedly helped sustain that morale.

5 Leadership

Superior leadership is often seen as the main reason for Union victory. Historians focus on several aspects of leadership.

a) Generalship

Northern commanders, while invariably outnumbering the enemy, had numerous difficulties to overcome, not least the fact that they had to move troops great distances into the South; defeat rebel armies; occupy enemy territory; subjugate the population; and maintain their supply lines. Northern generals, like Grant and Sherman finally rose to the occasion. Grant, an unpretentious but determined and implacable man, is often regarded as the greatest soldier of the war. He displayed his talent when capturing Fort Donelson in 1862 and Vicksburg in 1863.

Overall commander from March 1864, he brought rational direction to the Union cause. According to his supporters, he had a concept of the total-war strategy necessary to win the conflict, the skill to carry out that strategy, and the determination to keep pressing it despite the high cost in casualties. Historians have also sung the praises of Sherman. His marches through Georgia and the Carolinas, reaching parts of the Confederacy that the Confederate government thought couldn't be reached, weakened the South logistically, politically and psychologically.

Many charges have been brought against Confederate military leadership. It is often claimed that while the South had brilliant tactical leaders, it produced no generals who rose to the level of strategic vision demonstrated by Grant and Sherman. Robert E. Lee has particularly come in for criticism. His strategic vision, it has been claimed, was limited to the Virginia theatre, where his influence concentrated Confederate resources at the expense of the Western theatres. The result was that the Confederacy lost the West - and thus lost the war. The Western Confederate armies also suffered from inept generalship. The first overall Western commander, Albert Johnston, allowed Federal forces to break through the Tennessee and Cumberland river defence line early in 1862. Beauregard, Johnston's successor, tended to make plans not based on realities. Bragg quarrelled with everyone and had a dreadful record. Joe Johnston was popular with his men but refused to take chances and viewed with suspicion bordering on paranoia every action by the Richmond authorities that affected him or his army. Hood, who associated valour with high casualty rates, was responsible for a series of terrible defeats in 1864.

The Confederacy's command structure in the West was also a problem. There was an impossible tangle of authority and direction, so much so that it was not always clear who was in command. Internal feuds among the Western generals did not help matters. The result was that Confederate armies failed to develop a co-ordinated defence. President Davis ultimately bears responsibility for the overlapping command structure. He has also been blamed for interfering too much in military matters and for being responsible for the feuds that built up between himself and Generals Joe Johnston and Beauregard.

Confederate commanders are also charged with being too offensive-minded. Grade McWhiney and Perry Jamieson (who are particularly critical of Davis and Lee) have argued that the Confederacy literally bled itself to death in the first three years of the war by making costly attacks and losing their bravest men. They claim that the Confederates attacked in 8 of the first 12 big battles of the war, losing 97,000 men - 20,000 more than the Union. It is sometimes claimed that the Confederacy should not have tried to fight a conventional war at all. Perhaps if it had relied more on guerilla warfare, it might have eroded the Northern will to fight.

But claims that skilful Northern and incompetent Confederate military leadership explain the outcome of the Civil War are far from convincing. The Union army had more than its fair share of blunderers, especially in the Virginia theatre. Inept Northern leadership actually gave the Confederacy a chance of victory. The recent attacks on Lee have been overdone. Lee, a legend in and beyond his own lifetime, has become an obvious target for revisionist historians, anxious to establish their own reputations by knocking the so-called 'marble man' off his pedestal. But Lee deserves to be held in high regard. Despite being outnumbered in every major battle and campaign in which he fought, he won victories - victories which gave Southerners hope and dampened spirits in the North. Without Lee's generalship the Confederacy would have crumbled earlier. If other Confederate commanders had fought as well, the war might have had a different outcome.

The criticism that Davis and Lee paid too much attention to military operations in Virginia and not enough to those in the West is unfounded. It seems highly unlikely that the Confederacy could have won the war by concentrating most of its forces in the West where military conditions very much favoured the North. There was simply too much territory to defend and control of the major rivers gave the Union a colossal advantage. Virginia, the South's most important industrial state, had to be defended. In Virginia geographical conditions very much favoured the defender. The Army of Northern Virginia fought to defend a relatively small area, was able to draw upon the economic resources of Virginia and the Carolinas, and could make use of a number of rivers for defence purposes. The Confederacy, therefore, was right to concentrate its efforts in Virginia. Davis and Lee should be praised for so doing. It also made sense to send the best men and the best resources to the best army (the Army of Northern Virginia) and the best General (Lee!). Indeed Davis might be criticised, not so much for his preoccupation with Virginia, but instead for dividing scarce resources more or less equally between East and West. He might have been better diverting more manpower from West to East, as Lee urged. But Davis realised that the Confederacy could not survive long without both Virginia and the West. This was the dilemma. The Confederacy had not enough manpower to hold both areas. Davis hoped to use the Confederacy's interior lines of communications by ferrying forces from one front to another. This sometimes worked. But the South's poor railway system, which deteriorated as the war progressed, meant that the Confederacy was unable to use its interior lines of communication to good effect.

One reason the Confederate Western commanders did so badly was they faced some good Northern commanders - Grant, Sherman and Thomas. Another was the command structure, whereby Confederate territory and military resources were organised into administrative entities called departments, each with its own commanding officer.

Davis, aware of the co-ordination problems this caused, tried to provide better control by giving generals supervisory authority over several departments. But none of the unified command experiments worked. Davis was in part to blame: so too were the generals. But the sheer size of the West and the poor state of communications were the major problems. The department system seemed initially a useful mechanism to control military activity. Indeed, even with the benefit of hindsight, it is hard to think of a better system.

McWhiney and Jamieson's charge that Confederate commanders (and especially Lee) were too attack-minded is easy to refute. In fact, Union forces attacked more often than their Confederate opponents. Confederate commanders quickly recognised the advantage of fighting on the tactical defensive. (Lee, in 1862, was mockingly nicknamed 'King of Spades' because he ordered Confederate troops to dig defensive earthworks.) But Lee, like other Confederate commanders, was anxious to attack whenever possible. A purely defensive strategy would result in the Confederacy being picked off at will. The only hope, in Lee's view (and surely he was right) was to gamble; to retain the initiative; and to make use of the elan and spirit of his men. As Prussia was to prove in both the Seven Weeks War against Austria in 1866 and in the Franco-Prussian War of 1870-1, spectacular offensive victories could be won - despite the rifle-musket. On several occasions Lee's offensive strategy almost won him an annihilating victory . When he was finally forced on the defensive in 1864-5 and deprived of the opportunity to manoeuvre, he was unable to do the things he had done before: he had to fight the kind of fight he could not win.

The charge that the Confederacy failed to fight a guerilla war is mistaken. In many parts of the Confederacy there was bitter guerilla warfare. It was particularly nasty in Missouri where William Clarke Quantrill's 'bushwhackers' fought against Federal 'jayhawkers'. There was also guerilla activity in Kentucky, Florida, Tennessee, and Virginia. John Mosby - 'The Grey Ghost' - was the Confederacy's most daring guerilla leader in Northern Virginia. Here the guerilla war was relatively civilised, certainly compared with Missouri. Even so, guerilla war - an obvious way of disrupting Northern invasion and occupation - was becoming increasingly brutal across the South as a whole in 1864-5.

b) The Management of Military Supply

A second level where numerous historians have identified superior Northern leadership is in the management of military supply. Led by men like Secretary of War Stanton, Quartermaster General Meigs, Secretary of the Navy Gideon Welles and Chief of US Military Railways Herman Haupt, the North had developed by 1862 a group of top- and middle-level managers who organised the Union economy and the efficient flow of military and naval supplies. The Confederacy, it is claimed, could not match Northern skill in organisation. In this interpretation, it was not so much the North's greater resources but its better management of those resources that won the war.

However, Union superiority in the management of production and logistics has probably been overstated. While the North could undoubtedly draw on a wider field of entrepreneurial skills to mobilise men, resources, technology, industry and transportation, the Confederacy could boast some brilliant successes in this area of leadership. Ordnance Chief Josiah Gorgas built an arms and ammunition industry virtually from scratch and kept Confederate armies much better supplied than had seemed possible in 1861. From November 1862 until virtually the end of the war James Seddon and his assistant John Campbell ran the Confederate War Office with skill and efficiency. Secretary of the Navy Mallory was also bold and resourceful. Arguably the Confederacy did a great deal with very little and Southern administrative abilities went far toward keeping the Confederacy fighting for so long. The main problem was the shortage - not the management - of resources.

c) Diplomatic Skill

Only if Britain and France joined the war did the Confederacy have much chance of outright victory. It has been claimed that if the Confederacy had handled things correctly, Britain would have joined the war on the Confederate side. However, given that Prime Minister Palmerston did not wish to get involved in the conflict, it is difficult to see what more the Confederacy could have done. In the circumstances Union diplomats did not have to do a great deal to ensure that Britain remained neutral.

d) Managing the Economy and Finance

The Confederate government is usually charged with failing to efficiently manage the country's economy and finance. It is criticised, for example, for not taking control of the Southern railway network and for failing to use slaves to best effect. The main criticism, however, is that it printed far too much money, thus fuelling inflation, which ravaged the economy and lowered the morale of Southerners. However, it is easy to sympathise with the Confederate government. Given the lack of a trained bureaucracy, it was not in a position to mobilise the Southern economy for total war. Given the Northern blockade and the fact that the Confederacy had little specie, inflation was probably inevitable. Davis' government might have tried to raise more money by taxation - but ruinous taxes would probably have had just as damaging an effect on morale as runaway inflation. Given the economic imbalance between

North and South, it could be argued that the Confederacy managed its economic and financial affairs rather well. Somehow it managed to maintain over 3 per cent of its population under arms - a higher figure than the North. It is difficult to see what more the Confederacy could have done to deal with its main economic problem - the breakdown of its transportation system which made it difficult to get food supplies to both civilians and soldiers.

e) Lincoln and Davis

It is often claimed that Lincoln proved to be a far better leader than Davis. In 1960 David Potter went so far as to say: 'If the Union and Confederacy had exchanged presidents with one another, the Confederacy might have won its independence'. Lincoln is generally seen as more successful in communicating with the people, more skilful in keeping political factions working together for a common goal, and better able to endure criticism and work with his critics. He is lauded for keeping all his commanders (including Grant) on a leash, for appointing the final winning military team, for picking able administrative subordinates, and for knowing how to delegate. Davis, on the other hand, is often seen as austere, rigid, humourless and prone to making enemies: his feuds with two of his top generals, Beauregard and Joe Johnston, undoubtedly harmed the Southern war effort.

Lincoln's superiority to Davis might seem self-evident. But Lee could think of no Confederate leader who could have done a better job than Davis. And Lincoln did make mistakes. He went through six failures as commanders in the Virginia theatre before he found the right general. Some of his other military appointments and strategic decisions can also be criticised. It is worth remembering Wendell Phillips' view of him: 'He is a first-rate, second-rate man'.

6 Conclusion

By the winter of 1864-5 the military, social and political will of the Confederacy was drained. Soldiers deserted and were encouraged to do so by their families. Heavy losses, defeat in battle and the invasion and occupation of its territory had eroded the Southern will to resist. Lincoln's re-election in November 1864, itself largely the result of Union military success in September 1864, ended the hope that Northern morale might crack. Southerners, who had possessed spirit enough to engage in four years of terrible war, decided enough was enough. Southern morale collapsed chiefly because its armies were beaten in a series of campaigns and battles from mid-1863 onwards. If Confederate armies had continued to have had the same success on the battlefield as in the first two years of the war, it is unlikely that Southern morale would have collapsed. The Confederacy was finally beaten because they had fewer men and fewer resources. Grant in 1864-5 used the immense advantage of Northern numbers, military resources and money to good effect. These advantages had always been there: the Union just needed someone to ensure they were applied steadily and remorselessly. Grant did just that. But the main reason for his - and for Union - success was 'big battalions'. Unable to fight a perfect war, the Confederacy fell before the superior resources of the enemy.

Working on '*Conclusion: the Historiographical Debates*'

Your notes from this chapter should give you an understanding of historians' views about why the North won/South lost. You should appreciate by now that historians have a host of different opinions. My view is that the North, given its 'big battalions', was always favourite to win and that, in the circumstances, the South fought magnificently. (I also think Southerners were mad to go to war in the first place!) You should not meekly accept this view. Hopefully your notes should provide you with ammunition to challenge it!

Consider the following questions.

1 Did the North win or the South lose the American Civil War?
2 To what extent was poor leadership to blame for Confederate defeat in the Civil War?

While both questions ask you to explain why the war ended as it did, each requires you to tackle the issue in a different way. Consider each of the questions in turn. Try a 'brain-storming' session to pinpoint the various arguments you could put forward, and then go on to establish which ones you could argue effectively. When you have sorted out your views, try to work out a paragraph-by-paragraph plan for each question.

Question 1 asks you to decide whether Northern strengths or Southern weaknesses determined the outcome of the war. I think it was Union strength! That being the case I would probably first put forward the arguments for the opposite case - Confederate divisions, inferior leadership and loss of morale. Then - after an important 'However' or 'But' (two key words in all history essays) - I would go on to claim that it was the Union 'big battalions' which won the war. What would your conclusion be?

Question 2 is an interesting one. Which aspects of leadership - military, political, economic, diplomatic - are you going to focus on? Do you consider that poor leadership was to blame for Southern defeat? Or was the Confederacy so well led that, against all the odds, it succeeded in fighting a four-year war and even came close to victory?

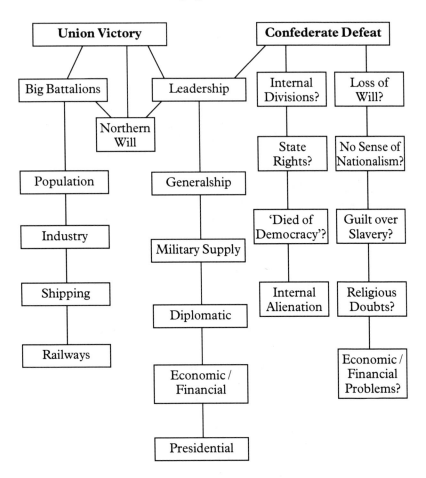

Summary - Conclusion: the Historiographical Debates

Chronological Table

1860 November   Election of President Lincoln
      December   South Carolina is the first of seven states to secede

1861 February   The Confederacy established at Montgomery
                           Jefferson Davis inaugurated Confederate President
      March   Lincoln inaugurated President of the USA
      April   Confederates attack Fort Sumter. Virginia seceded
      July   First battle of Manassas (Bull Run)

1862 February   Union capture of Fort Henry and Fort Donelson
      March   Battle of Shiloh
      April   Confederates introduced conscription
      April   Union navy captured New Orleans
      June   Robert E. Lee took command of the Army of
                       Northern Virginia
      June-July   Seven Days Battles
      August   Second Manassas
      September   Battle of Antietam
      September   Lincoln issued Emancipation Proclamation
      December   Battle of Fredericksburg

1863 March   Union government enacted conscription
      May   Battle of Chancellorsville
      May   Death of Stonewall Jackson
      July   Battle of Gettysburg.
      July   Fall of Vicksburg
      July   New York draft riots
      September   Battle of Chickamauga
      November   Lincoln's Gettysburg Address
      November   Battles of Lookout Mountain and Missionary Ridge

1864 May-June   Campaign from Wilderness to Petersburg
      June   Siege of Petersburg began
      September   Capture of Atlanta
      November   Lincoln re-elected President
      November   Sherman began march from Atlanta to the sea
      December   Sherman captured Savannah
      December   Battle of Nashville

1865 February   Sherman began march through the Carolinas
      April   Fall of Petersburg and Richmond
      April   Lee surrendered at Appomattox
      April   Assassination of Lincoln.

Further Reading

You will not be surprised to learn that there are hundreds of excellent books on the American Civil War, including some of the finest works of American history ever written. This list offers only a brief sample of some of the most significant works. It is unlikely that you will have time to consult more than just a few of these. However, it is vital that you read some, particularly if you are taking the topic as a special or depth study. The topic is one of considerable controversy and you will be in a better position to form your own conclusions if you have read widely. The following suggestions are meant to serve as a guide from which you might wish to 'pick and mix'.

1 General Texts. There are many general works that cover the war (and its causes). **J.M. McPherson,** *Battle Cry of Freedom,* (Penguin 1988) remains the best one-volume survey of the causes and course of the Civil War. **R.M. Sewell,** *A House Divided: Sectionalism and Civil War, 1848-1865,* (John Hopkins University Press 1988) is a more succinct account. **P.J. Parish,** *The American Civil War,* (Holmes and Meier 1975) remains an essential text. **A. Nevins,** *The War for the Union* (4 vols Charles Scribner's Sons 1959-71) is a masterpiece but probably too detailed for most readers. **B. Catton,** *Centennial History of the Civil War* (3 vols, 1961-8) traces the war's military progress in vivid prose. **S. Foote,** *The Civil War,* (3 vols 1958-74) is splendid but even more detailed than Nevins and Catton!

2 The Nature of the War. Perhaps the two best books covering the general nature of the war are: **B.I. Wiley,** *The Life of Johnny Reb: The Common Soldier of the Confederacy,* (Bobbs-Merrill 1943). **B.I. Wiley,** *The Life of Billy Yank: The Common Soldier of the Union,* (Bobbs-Merrill 1943). The fact that both these books are still in print is testimony to their readabilty and scholarship. The following texts are also worth reading: **G.F. Linderman,** *The Experience of Combat in the American Civil War,* (The Free Press 1987) **A. Jones,** *Civil War Command and Strategy,* (Macmillan 1992) **J.M. McPherson,** *What Men Fought For,* (Oxford University Press 1992)

3 Military Events. The military events are well covered in the general texts mentioned above. The following books are also worth consulting. **H. Hattaway and A. Jones,** *How the North Won,* (University of Illinois Press 1983) **R.M. McMurry,** *Two Great Rebel Armies: An Essay in Confederate Militay History* (University of North Carolina Press 1989) **M.C.C. Adams,** *Fighting for Defeat: Union Military Failure in the East 1861-1865,* (University of Nebraska Press 1992) **J.J. Hennessy,** *Return to Bull Run,* (Simon and Schuster 1993) **S.W. Sears,** *To the Gates of Richmond,* (Ticknor and Fields 1992)

4 The Confederacy at War. **R.N. Current** (ed), *The Encylopedia of the Confederacy* (4 vols Simon and Schuster 1993) is the essential text. It is a collection of essays on every conceivable topic and person by all the best historians. No library should be without this! The following are also useful: **E.M. Thomas,** *The Confederate Nation 1861-5,* (Harper and Row 1979) **E.M. Coulter,** *The Confederate States of America, 1861-1865,* (Louisiana State University Press 1950) **C. Eaton,** *A History of the Southern Confederacy,* (The Free Press 1954) **P.D. Escott,** *After Secession: Jefferson Davis and the Failure of Confederate Nationalism* (Louisiana State University Press 1978) **G.C. Rable,** *Civil Wars: Women and the*

Crisis of Southern Nationalism, (University of Illinois Press 1989)

5 The Northern Home Front. Unfortunately, there is not an Encyclopedia of the Union. (One day there is sure to be!) **P.S. Paludan,** *A People's Contest: The Union and Civil War 18561-1865,* (Harper and Row 1988) is a good survey of the impact of the war on Northern society. **P.S. Paludan,** *The Presidency of Abraham Lincoln,* (University of Kansas 1994) looks at all aspects of Lincoln's work as President. **M.E. Neely Jr,** *The Fate of Liberty* (Oxford University Press 1991) examines the issue of civil liberties in the North during the war. **M.E. Neely Jr,** *The Abraham Linoln Encylopedia,* (McGraw-Hill 1982) remains a very useful work.

6 The Destruction of Slavery. I. Berlin *et al,* eds, *Freedom: A Documentary History of Emancipation, 1861-1867,* Series 1, Volume 1: The Destruction of Slavery, (Cambridge University Press 1985) is perhaps the most relevant work of a massively conceived series. **I. Berlin** (*et al*), *Slaves No More,* (Cambridge University Press 1992) contains some distilled wisdom from *Freedom: A Documentary History of Emancipation.* **J.T. Glatthaar,** *Forged in Battle: The Civil War Alliance of Black Soldiers and White Officers,* (Free Press 1990) examines the role of the black soldier. **J.M. McPherson,** *The Struggle for Equality: Abolitionists and the Negro in the Civil War and Reconstruction* (Princeton Paberbacks 1964) has recently been republished.

7 Britain and the Civil War. There are relatively few books dealing with the foreign dimension. **H. Jones,** *Union in Peril,* (University of North Carolina 1992) is the most accessible.

8 Why the North Won. Three volumes are essential. **D. Donald** (ed), *Why the North Won the Civil War,* (Collier 1960) - a superb collection of essays providing different explanations for the war's outcome. **R.E Beringer, H. Hattaway, A. Jones and W.N. Still Jr,** *Why the South Lost the Civil War,* (University of Georgia Press 1986) and **G.S. Boritt** (ed), *Why the Confederacy Lost,* (Oxford University Press 1992).

9 Biographies. One of the best ways to get a deeper understanding of actions and ideas is through biography. Fortunately a large number of first-rate biographies exist of many of the leading figures involved in the Civil War. These include: **D. Donald,** *Lincoln* (Cape 1995) **S.B. Oates,** *With Malice Toward None: The Life of Abraham Lincoln,* (Mentor 1977) **M.E. Neely, Jr,** *The Last Best Hope of Earth: Abraham Lincoln and the Promise of America,* (Harvard University Press 1993) **A.T. Nolan,** *Lee Considered: General Robert E. Lee in Civil War History,* (University of North Carolina Press 1991) **W.S. McFeely,** *Grant,* (Norton 1982) **J.F. Marszalek,** *Sherman: A Soldier's Passion for Order,* (Free Press 1993)

10 Primary Material. Many collections/volumes of primary material are available. Among the most useful are: **H.S. Commager** (ed), *The Blue and the Gray,* (Wings Books 1950) **R.U. Johnson and C.C. Buel** (eds), *Battles and Leaders of the Civil War* (4 vols Castle 1887) **U.S. Grant,** *Memoirs and Selected Letters,* (Library of America 1990) **C. Vann Woodward** (ed), *Mary Chesnut's Civil War,* (Yale University Press 1981)

11 More Specialist Works

Students who wish to track down more specialist works can most effectively start via the bibliographies in **J.M. McPherson's** (1988) volume and in *The Encyclopedia of the Confederacy* (1993).

Index